Kindness is Contagious

100 Stories to Remind You

God is Good

and

So are Most People

by

Nicole J. Phillips

Table of Contents

Introduction

The publisher of The Forum Newspaper in Fargo, North Dakota called me mid-summer of 2011 and offered me the opportunity of a lifetime: the chance to write about anything I wanted for the launch of a new section of the paper.

I was flattered and scared to death. *Didn't he know I was a television anchor, not a newspaper columnist? What could I possibly write about week after week that would hold my own attention, not to mention the fragile attention of the Forum readers?*

The publisher suggested politics. I politely but vehemently declined. He recommended cooking. I sheepishly admitted I had made lasagna twice and forgotten to put in the lasagna noodles both times. He proposed parenting and I said, "Absolutely! That will be perfect... once I figure out how to do it."

I spent nearly a month searching my soul trying to figure out what I could write about each week. The answer was given to me by a girl in a gold bikini.

Gold Bikini Girl is the first story in this book, and the first column I ever wrote for the paper. My encounter with the young woman in the story helped me find my purpose and changed the trajectory of my life. It turned me into a writer.

I had always hoped I'd have the chance to thank her, and due to my husband and a McDonald's PlayPlace, I did.

About a year after I started the column, my husband called me with a flurry of words.

Saul: Nic, I'm at McDonald's and I see Gold Bikini Girl!

Me: How do you know it's her? Is she wearing a gold bikini?

Saul: No! I'm serious! She's here with a little girl and she's just the way you described her. It's gotta be her.

Saul had eavesdropped well enough to find out that this mystery woman came to the restaurant every Tuesday after a mother-child class at the local YMCA.

I'm sure you can guess, the next Tuesday I was camped out at McDonald's waiting for her. My husband was right. It was Gold Bikini Girl.

It took me a while to get up the nerve to talk to her. I finally introduced myself and told her about the column. She had never seen it, so I pulled it up on my phone.

As I started reading our story aloud, I was a little embarrassed by the number of times I had referred to her as Gold Bikini Girl in the newspaper. She said she remembered that sunny afternoon at the pool, but I regret now not asking her to share her version of the day.

In the end, we both ended up with tears in our eyes as I thanked her for helping me find my passion. I never saw my beautiful blond-haired friend again. I often wonder what she's doing, or more accurately, how she's doing. I hope God blesses her wildly for playing such an important role in helping me find my voice.

Acts of kindness are often done and forgotten. They become cute stories we pull out once in awhile to remind ourselves this planet is smaller than we think or that good people exist in a sometimes bad world.

While all of these articles have previously appeared in the newspaper, I began feeling called to unearth them once again for a book when I realized the cumulative effect they have had on my own life. It is my hope that people who read these stories back-to-back will realize the immense potential of kindness and be moved to begin their own altruistic life journey.

I am certain kindness has the power to transform your life because I have seen it transform mine.

Gold Bikini Girl

I've heard it's sinful to do something nice and then tell everyone about it. Well, hopefully the Man Upstairs will forgive me for this.

This past summer I was at the Fargo North pool with my three kids. We walk in, and my 7-year-old daughter chooses the one lounge chair situated right next to an 18-year-old beauty in a shiny gold bikini. Wearing my one piece swimsuit with a head-to-toe cover-up, this is not exactly my idea of an ideal location. Alas, I was hoping there wouldn't be an impromptu Fairest of the Pool Pageant.

My 15-month-old son starts sharing Cheerios with the 15-month-old girl being watched by Gold Bikini Girl. I put my jealousy of her gorgeousness aside and start talking to the woman. The kids were born a week apart. The little girl, Audrey, begins using sign language to say "more" and "thank you." The woman tells me she's been teaching Audrey signs for more than a year.

After more conversation, I learn all sorts of things about Gold Bikini Girl. She is actually the mom of Audrey (um, how do you go through childbirth and still rock a bikini?!). She is raising her daughter on her own and living in a nearby apartment.

Before we left the pool that day I felt compelled to tell Gold Bikini Girl just what an amazing mom I think she is. She was so engaged in her daughter's life. I have a husband to help co-parent, and I still barely have the energy to make it out of the house. Wow. We should all have it so totally together.

As I walked to my nearly new minivan, I saw the woman walk to the other side of the parking lot to a compact car that had probably seen many previous owners. My heart told me to stop. I reached into my purse and pulled out some cash.

I drove over to the woman and interrupted her while she was buckling up little Audrey. My words went something like this: "I don't know you, but I need to tell you something. When I was 30, my best friend, Heather, died of cancer. Heather always believed in the power of people to lift each other up. Each month, in honor of Heather, I give to someone who touches my soul – someone who may be going through a tough time, but who will overcome. I believe you will do amazing things with your life. Please take this money and know that you have touched my heart."

The woman burst into tears. I think she was grateful that instead of receiving a nod of disapproval, she was getting a pat on the back.

But guess what? I got WAY more out of it than she did. I walked around for days thinking about how this young mother had inspired me with her courage and grace.

It's hard to write about giving without sounding self-righteous, but the bottom line is this. I want people to feel the way I felt.

Here's where you come in. These stories of kindness are everywhere. Since moving to Fargo, I have been on the receiving end too many times to count. The downfall of being from a place where we are so humble is that we don't get to feel the joy that comes from sharing and reliving the experience of giving.

I want you to share your stories with me. Stories of times you've done something nice for a total stranger or stories of times someone has gone out of their way to help you. If kind works set into motion other acts of kindness, imagine how amazing this life could be.

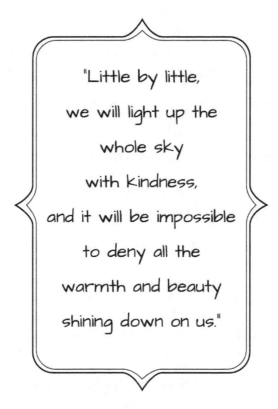

"Little by little,

we will light up the

whole sky

with kindness,

and it will be impossible

to deny all the

warmth and beauty

shining down on us."

What are You Looking At?

Have you ever noticed that when you get something stuck in your mind you start seeing it everywhere?

When I gave up drinking, every billboard I drove past for at least a month was advertising some sort of alcoholic beverage. When Saul and I started thinking about getting a security system for the new house, it seemed like we had a non-stop loop of ADT commercials on our television and every story on the news was about a home burglary.

Life seems to work like that. Whatever we focus on becomes bigger.

So today I'd like to ask, what are you looking at?

Is it ISIS, domestic violence, human trafficking, poverty, hunger or just plain evil in general?

Or is it love? And kindness? And beauty amid the troubles surrounding us?

If your mind is on the decay of our society, you will notice that our society is decaying. If your mind is trained to zero-in on the tiny acts of kindness lighting up a very dark world, you will notice the light.

I use the word "trained" because that's how it worked for me. I've been writing this column since 2011. When I began, I had to intentionally look for acts of kindness (and then pounce on the people involved) so I had something to write about each Saturday.

Very quickly, my mind became "trained" to notice people holding open doors, speaking kindly in contentious situations and going out of their way to help wherever it was needed.

Then I took the next step. When I wasn't seeing kindness, I created it, and kindness became the key that unlocked forgiveness, passion and healing in my life. I believe it continues to keep me healthy, which is why it's so important to me to keep it at the forefront of my mind.

As much as I focus on kindness, I'm starting to notice a disappointing trend. People around me are becoming scared and discouraged. They seem to feel the darkness closing in around them and are thinking that the little they can do for others will never be enough.

I don't see it that way. When I close my eyes, I see all of the people on Earth standing and staring at the sky. Only they aren't looking at the real sky, they are looking at a huge black tarp blocking out the light. Each time someone does an act of kindness, a tiny pin-sized hole is poked into that big, black tarp, allowing in a speck of light.

Someone notices the light and does another act of kindness, creating yet another little hole. Someone sees that new light, realizes what is happening and starts creating more little openings for light through their own acts of kindness.

I see my job, through writing this column, as pushing my fingernails through those pin-sized holes and ripping them open with all of my might. I want to allow in as much light as possible, by drawing attention to the acts of kindness being done.

That's why I love it when people share with me the kindness they see around them, because it gives me the chance to rip open that tiny dot of light and share it with many more people.

Little by little, we will light up the whole sky with kindness, and it will be impossible to deny all the warmth and beauty shining down on us.

But the question remains, as you stand there, looking up at that big black tarp, what do you see? Darkness? Or light? Your focus makes all the difference.

How Kindness Healed Me

I recently realized I've been writing this column for almost exactly two years. I still remember standing on stage at The Avalon in downtown Fargo for the launch party of the new SheSays section. I felt so proud to be included in such a prominent group of female writers and more than a little overwhelmed and intimidated.

I was nervous writing about kindness. I wasn't sure people would buy into the whole "we sure could use a little good news" thing that worked so well for Anne Murray.

There have been times over the past two years when my email inbox has been flooded with stories of kindness; other times it has been a deserted wasteland of spam.

I have seen growth in my writing and learned to deal with criticism. I feel a new level of comfort in sharing my opinions and personal stories.

I probably could have predicted those changes if I had ever stopped long enough to think about them. What I never could have anticipated are the ways in which I have changed physically and mentally since dedicating my life to kindness.

Researcher Allan Luks did a study in the 1990s involving more than 3,000 men and women. He concluded that regular helpers are 10 times more likely to be in good health than people who don't volunteer.

Another study by the federal government in 2007 found that people ages 65 and older actually live longer and have lower rates of depression when they volunteer.

That was interesting to me because several years ago, I was a Lexapro junkie. OK, maybe not a true junkie, but I did rely on the drug to control my depression and anxiety.

Around the time I started looking for acts of kindness to do, I decided to try life medication-free. It was a gamble. I have three kids who need their momma to keep it together. I never had that crawl-under-the-covers-for-days sort of depression, but everyone around me could definitely tell when I was feeling off.

I weaned off the Lexapro. The first time I felt the dark cloud coming over me, instead of turning to a pill, I tried turning toward kindness. I made a distinct effort to do a random act of kindness for a stranger.

All of a sudden, I felt a huge rush of adrenaline, a blast of energy and total exhilaration. Several hours later, a heightened sense of calm and emotional well-being overtook my body.

I had experienced what Luks defined as the "helper's high."

According to Luks, the high has a biochemical explanation. Volunteering (or in my case a random act of kindness) reduces the body's stress and releases endorphins, the brain's natural painkillers.

Luks found stress-related health problems improve after performing kind acts. A drop in stress may, for some people, even decrease the constriction within the lungs that leads to asthma attacks.

Helping can decrease both the intensity and the awareness of physical pain in the body. It can strengthen the immune system.

Helping reverses feelings of depression from stress, supplies social contact and decreases feelings of hostility and isolation that can cause overeating and ulcers.

I don't know if you've noticed, but a few months ago I

updated my column photo. I've lost about 30 pounds since 2011, and thanks to Forum photographer Carrie Snyder, I have been able to exchange head shots. It turns out Luks may have been right about that overeating part.

Kindness is contagious, but I think it is also reparative. As soon as I started focusing on other people more than myself, I began healing myself.

Kindness and even the act of looking for acts of kindness got me out of my own head. I stopped focusing on me and in return I was the biggest beneficiary of any act of kindness I could have ever delivered.

Judy's Charity

I am officially afraid to open my email.

I come from the world of television news. If you didn't like how I looked, what I said or how I was saying it, you turned to your husband and complained to him. I seldom got to hear feedback from viewers.

Apparently the newspaper world is a whole different game. I never imagined that when I asked readers to write me, they actually would. I am overwhelmed by all the stories of kindness. They are captivating, and each one is filled with real-life characters I want to meet.

And yes, I'm afraid to open my email in front of anyone because I know there's a good chance it contains yet another story that will bring me to tears, like this one from Judy, who lives in Fargo:

"Nicole, I'm sure in a community like ours you are getting flooded with stories of acts of kindness by others.

"One that sticks out in my mind the most is from back in 1993. I was working at the Roger Maris Cancer Center, and I was a single mom. I had been single for 11 years, and my daughter, Charity, was 12 years old at the time. She was diagnosed at the age of 4 with dilated cardiomyopathy.

"She was on medication, and none of her friends knew anything, but the people I worked with did. They knew if I got a call that was urgent, I would need to leave immediately.

"During that time, I needed to get a test on my heart just to see if Charity's condition was somehow inherited. They didn't find cardiomyopathy, but they did find a 1½-inch hole in my heart. The doctor said I should have it operated on soon.

"The problem was that Charity's heart function had gotten worse and they wanted to put her through the strenuous testing for a heart transplant around the time I would be operated on. I had just bought a house over in Moorhead six months before my diagnosis. I knew I would probably lose my house now as I had to miss a week of work for Charity's test and I didn't know how long I would be out for my surgery.

"Before my surgery, the director of the Cancer Center asked me to stop into her office. There, on her desk, was a bag of cards. She told me to take them home and read them if I could before my surgery. So that night I sat at my table and opened every card with Charity at my side. Every one of those cards had money in it and words of prayer and good will. I had enough money to make three house payments.

"I went into surgery with not an ounce of worry about losing my house. I knew that I was taken care of, not just by God and Charity, but by the wonderful people I worked with, and for that I am eternally grateful."

Because Kindness Matters

"What would Nicole do?" I honestly had a women tell me she thought those words to herself as she watched a man try to pile an entire load of dumped lumber back into his pickup, in the rain, in the middle of 45th Street.

Um ... maybe I gave you the wrong idea. I don't always do the right thing. But I love hearing about people who do. So to Sarah, who stood in a downpour in front of Space Aliens to help a stranger pile up two-by-fours, let me say, I'm so thankful to hear you caught the Kindness Bug instead of pneumonia.

Sarah's 10 year-old son was there to witness the whole thing. What an amazing example she set. Just like Beth, who sent me this email:

"It was so heartwarming to read your article in the Fargo Forum. I connected with you immediately, because part of my daily routine as a teacher (and mother) is to teach my students the importance of random acts of kindness on a daily basis. At the bottom signature of my emails, one will see the words 'because Kindness Matters,' and the signature of my text messages on my cellphone reads 'because nice matters.'

"The purpose of both signatures (in my technology world) is to hopefully remind people of what is important in life. I, too, am not one to tell others about something nice I did for someone, but this random act of kindness keeps resurfacing to warm my heart and influence my children.

"Two years ago during the flood fight, I was at the JCPenney hair salon about to purchase $45 in hair products for myself. Ahead of me were two soldiers from the Guard who had come in to get haircuts during their break of building dikes to save our flooding community. After the gentlemen were brought to the back of the salon for their cuts, I put all my hair products back on the shelf and told the cashier that I wanted to pay for the soldiers' haircuts.

"With a surprised look on her face, she asked me, 'Are you serious?'

" 'Absolutely,' I responded. 'I can do without styling products for a couple months, but we can't beat the flood without the soldiers.'

"The gal behind the counter asked if she could tell them my name. I told her, 'No, thank you. Just tell them thank you for all they do.' My gesture felt so small compared to what they do for us every day. But the impact it left on my 7 year old son standing next to me and the cashier behind the counter, began a chain reaction of kindness.

"As we left the store empty handed, the little boy holding my hand smiled and said, 'Wow, Mom, that was cool. I bet they will be so happy!'

"When I returned to the salon a couple of months later, this time with all three of my boys, the lady at the desk remembered me immediately. She smiled and said to my sons, 'Do you know how kind your mom is? What she did for two strangers one day reminded me to go out of my way to help others.' My boys smiled, and my oldest son replied with, 'Yeah, thanks. We know.'

"It wasn't a pat on the back I was hoping to get; it was the example it set for my sons and three perfect strangers … a chain reaction. Not to mention, it felt good to do it because it made someone else happy."

Letter of Love

I love it when life knocks you over the head. That happened to me this week. I was struggling to write this column. I have a few other things going on in my life: my husband was out of town, I took my kids to Minneapolis for the weekend, my husband came home, I ended up sick in bed, I felt guilty for ignoring my kids while I was sick in bed, and the laundry just kept piling up. You know the story. It's life. It happens to all of us.

So here I am mustering up the energy to write this column when a total stranger gives me the greatest gift of kindness. She sent me a letter.

Laverne, from North Fargo, sent me the letter in response to my column last week. She was specifically referring to this comment I wrote in the Letter of Love to my daughter, Jordan: "Even when I'm acting ugly, running around the house throwing a tantrum because something didn't get done fast enough, you show me kindness."

Here's Laverne's Letter of Love that had me sitting in front of my computer with tears streaming down my face.

"Dear Nicole,

I can't wait for Saturday mornings to get the paper and read your article. Today, I laughed and shed tears as I read. You ugly? I doubt it. Maybe mismatched for the day, but not ugly. Do I ever remember those days when I had two very bright, well-adjusted teenagers, an adopted child with multiple needs, an insane dog, and a husband on the road.

Forget the jam on the floor, the unmade beds, the crumbs in the sheets. The kids will not remember those 'unacceptable' situations, but they will remember when you listened to them, understood their fears and anxieties, hugged them, and accepted them for who and what they were striving to be. When they grow up they will remember and thank God for the best mom in the whole universe.

I send your articles to my cousin in California for a day brightener as she struggles with Parkinson's.

Come quick, Saturday Morning.

Laverne"

Thank you so much Laverne for making me feel like what I do, in all areas of my life, has value. And thank you Life, for knocking me over the head and reminding me there are so many ways to show kindness.

Slow Down and Spread Some Kindness

How many times do we run into the same people over and over again and yet still never get to know them?

Maybe you can tell me a lot about your hairdresser, but what about the man who rings you up every other week at the gas station? Or the woman who makes you coffee on Monday mornings? Or the person who hands over your dry cleaning a few times a month?

Who are they? Does it even matter? This story of kindness sent in by Jamie in Glyndon, MN proves that it does.

"Over the years, my mother-in-law, Chris, has gotten to know the mechanic at the car dealership where she services her vehicle pretty well. A few months ago he was in a car accident and hurt fairly badly. She took the time to pay him a visit to see how he was doing and bring him a plant.

Fast forward a few months... She and her son, Dave, and another friend of ours were at our lake cabin moving some stuff around. She had been telling Dave that she really needed to stop in and say hi to the mechanic again. She was concerned about him and wanted to see how he was recovering. They thought maybe they would stop by on their way home. After they finished cleaning up at the cabin they stopped at a restaurant for supper. Instead of bringing the three of them the check, their waitress brought them a message: Their bill had been taken care of by a man dining in the same restaurant.

Lo and behold, the guy who had paid for their dinner was the mechanic, the one who had been hurt and the one they were planning to visit.

When my mother-in-law went over to thank him, she ended up getting the thanks. The mechanic told her that she was the only person who had taken the time to check in on him after his accident. He said he appreciated it so much that the least he felt he could do was to buy her supper."

This story reminds me that even when I feel crabby, preoccupied or way too rushed to start a conversation with every person I see, it's important to slow down.

Taking the time to look someone in the eyes, ask how he or she is doing and then actually waiting to hear the response is important. It's a way to show someone kindness. It doesn't cost anything, but to the person receiving that extra moment of your time, it could be priceless.

As you work on your New Year's Resolutions to eat right, wear your seatbelt and call your mother more often, I hope you will work on this one too: Slow down and spread kindness.

A Football Team to the Rescue

Every year, Mother Nature seems to do her best to force us to show kindness to each other. Who knows how she will get to us this year, maybe a blizzard, maybe a flood, maybe both.

A North Fargo woman sent me this story, reminding me how nice it is to know that regardless of what comes our way, we can count on each other.

"Sunday morning, Aug. 27, 2007, my parents got up and went to church to be greeted with the terrible news that their pastor had unexpectedly died during the night. In his mid-forties, my parents considered Pastor Bill their fourth child. Bad got worse, because that evening, the tornado sirens went off.

"My parents' home was one of the first houses to be destroyed in the worst tornado Northwood, North Dakota has ever experienced. What was left of their house was quickly destroyed by the rain that fell right after the tornado.

"Despite the danger of the situation, injuries some experienced and concern about my parents' safety, an absurd thought came to mind – my wedding dress is in my parents' basement! I need to get it out before it's destroyed! It's strange what one thinks of in an emergency.

"The following week was a numbing blur for my parents, both in their early 70s, as we began the process of salvaging what could be saved, adding to the growing pile of rubbish in the front yard, and allowing the generosity of strangers to feed us and force us to take much-needed breaks (Thank you, Salvation Army).

"The Community Center was filled to capacity within a day or two with food, paper products, toiletries, hand-made quilts, clothing and anything else you could imagine one would need who suddenly had no home.

"Pastor Bill's funeral was held six days after the tornado — the same day that my parents needed to finish demolishing their house and get it to the rubbish pile so the city could haul it away. Time wasn't on their side, but attending the funeral was important to my parents, so we went.

"We left my husband, son, niece and nephew, along with one hammer and two crowbars, to complete the impossibly large task of getting the house to the curb.

"It turns out they weren't going to have to do it alone. As they started to work, a bus pulled up filled with young, well-rested, strong University of North Dakota football players.

"No tools needed, those athletes picked up a chimney weighing several hundred pounds and threw it onto the pile, used their fists and bare hands to remove walls and hauled out furniture and wet carpet in bucket-brigade fashion.

"Two hours later they disappeared as quickly as they came, without fanfare or accolades, with my husband staring in disbelief at what had been accomplished.

"The following day, back at church in Fargo, our pastor asked the congregation if anyone wanted to contribute to my parents' needs. That day about 30 people gave nearly $1,400 to a couple many had never met. I received cash to give to my parents from people at the grocery store, from other parents at school functions and even at the homecoming coronation at Fargo North High School.

"Others donated their time and manpower.

"The town of Northwood has nearly been restored. Much good has come out of this tragedy, one of them being a home that is handicap-accessible for my aging parents.

"But more importantly, discovering that despite what we hear on the news, people care and want to help. People that need help can be open to receiving it, which seems to always give them a 'pay it forward' attitude. And the 'side-line' people, like myself, can be blown away by the generosity and genuine concern of people, whether friends, neighbors, or total strangers.

"Several years later, I am still humbled by those who were there with goods, donations or to make sure my wedding dress made it out, safe and sound."

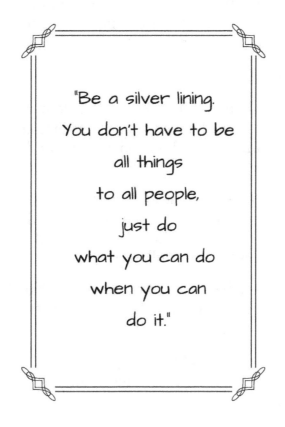

"Be a silver lining.
You don't have to be
all things
to all people,
just do
what you can do
when you can
do it."

Act Like a Child

I love my kids. In fact, I love all kids. Especially the littlest ones, who see things that I used to see, but for some reason I miss now that I'm all grown up.

This story from Lana Schlecht, a dentist in Ellendale, N.D., reminds me that it often takes a child to see what the rest of us are missing.

"Dear Nicole,

"Sometimes a chance encounter opens a door. I was at my hairdresser when she happened to mention that her daughter's second-grade class had a student missing one day.

"The milk break came in the afternoon and since one person was missing, the milk was given to a student whose family could not afford to buy it. The child always sat and watched the others have a snack of milk or juice.

"My hairdresser's little daughter exclaimed that she wished the child could get milk every day since that student was so very happy to finally be included.

"I grew up very poor, so I have a real heart for those kids. The situation they are in is not their fault, but they can't do anything about it.

"As an adult, I can finally help. I got my church involved, and we took this on as a project. No child is now excluded from milk break. If a family can't afford the snack, we provide it for them.

"Nutrition is vitally important for these little ones. If my hairdresser had not been touched by the situation told to her by her own little girl, the problem would still be around."

It took the eyes of a child to notice someone hurting, someone left out, someone feeling different because of their lot in life.

Do you remember how touched you were by the little things in life when you were a child? It's childhood innocence, but it's also childhood intellect.

The little people in our lives know enough to giggle when something is funny, stomp their feet when someone is ignoring them or wave "hi" when someone else is being ignored.

Imagine how fulfilled your life could be if you started acting like a child. Maybe you don't need to stomp your feet to get your boss to pay attention to your great ideas at work, but you could try waving at a stranger who looks like he or she might need a friend. Imagine how quickly that act of kindness could catch on.

I ask my kids every day after school, "What was your act of kindness today?" Sometimes they shared a swing, sometimes they helped pick up dropped papers, sometimes they admit they still have to work on one that day.

Kindness doesn't have to be big, just consistent. If you can't figure out anything nice to do, ask a child. They are full of ideas.

A Full Tank and an Empty Purse

Have you ever experienced one of those totally uncomfortable moments where everyone is standing around and no one knows quite what to say?

It's happened to me ... when my credit card is inexplicably denied at the grocery store. I want to shout to everyone in line behind me, "I PAY MY BILLS! I SWEAR!" but perhaps that month I had forgotten.

It's happened to me ... when the woman in front of me has to tell the cashier to put back the cereal box because she didn't realize the bill would be so high.

Those situations are awkward, but as Barton Cahill from Moorhead demonstrates with his story, they are also incredible opportunities to show kindness.

"Nicole, Love your column. It reminded me of something that happened last spring when I was visiting the Twin Cities.

"I went to a gas station, filled up my tank, and went inside to pay. I was waiting in line, along with a number of other customers, many of whom looked grumpy and impatient.

"The first lady in line was looking in her purse, and suddenly realized she had no money or credit cards with her to pay the cashier. We all saw what was going on, and without really thinking, I went up to her and told her I would be happy to pay for her gas.

"She was flabbergasted, as were the others waiting in line. She initially refused, but I insisted on paying. She wanted my phone number and address to pay me back later. I told her 'Don't worry about it. I don't want you to pay me back.' She finally talked me into giving her my information.

34

"We parted ways, and I can tell you what happened that day probably lifted my spirits more than it helped her pay for a tank of gas. I experienced that wonderful feeling you spoke of in your column.

"Sure enough, the lady soon sent me a beautiful thank-you card, along with a check for the money I had given her that day. And even better, that little incident is likely something both of us will remember for a long time, maybe forever."

Barton, I would be willing to bet there was a whole convenience store full of people who went home and shared that story with their families. Maybe it even sparked the urge in them to leave their comfort zones and carry on with kindness, thanks to your example.

Living Their Faith by Giving

There's a church in town giving away money. If the idea of eternal riches won't get you through the door, then maybe cold, hard cash will.

Twice this past year, Ignite Church in Moorhead passed out a gift to its members. Each member got an envelope filled with cash – $10, $20, $50 or $100. But the cash wasn't the gift. The real gift was the experience of giving that money to someone else, someone in need.

I'm starting to hear about all of the ways people are choosing to share that money. The stories are invigorating and inspiring. Here are a few:

Passing on the blessing

"The four people in my family each got $20 in our envelopes. We decided to put it all together.

After praying about it, we decided that we would go to WalMart on Christmas Eve and ask God to direct us to the person we should give it to. As we walked around, we saw a young mother with three children. A little later we saw her again.

We went up and told her how God had blessed us this Christmas season and that we wanted to be a blessing to her. We handed her the envelope and chatted a bit. She told us they were trying to have a merry Christmas, but her dad works for American Crystal Sugar and there was a strike so he was locked out of his job.

We talked about her kids a bit, and in the conversation she mentioned that she only shops for clothes at thrift stores. Those two things really made us feel that we had found the right person to be a blessing to.

We wished her a Merry Christmas and went on our way. It felt really good to be able to help someone out, especially at Christmastime."

A holiday feast

"We were able to bless four different families by paying for their meals at various restaurants. This not only blessed the families, but the restaurant staff, too.

They were in awe of someone doing such a thing in the name of Jesus and the spirit of Christmas giving. We asked that they not tell who did the act of kindness, but to simply say 'Someone wishes you a Merry Christmas!'"

Selfless giving

"The young gentleman we brought with us to Ignite Church had never been to a church before. He was so excited to get an envelope and learn the reason behind the gesture.

His mother had just been laid off and told him and his brother that morning that they didn't have money for Christmas gifts. This young man took the funds in his envelope and purchased a gift for his dad, his mom, and his brother and NOTHING for himself.

He said he couldn't wait to see his mom's face when he told her of the service and what the church is doing for other people."

A much-needed breather

"My husband and I had been given $30. We knew there would be someone with a need and had been keeping our eye out for that special situation.

One Sunday at church a young mom with a newborn came

and asked for prayer. She was so stressed and exhausted from meeting everyone's needs and taking care of her third child. The biggest weight was the cost of child care as she was going back to work in a couple weeks. I told her I would come and babysit so she could get a breather.

When I saw her again the next Sunday, I still felt that small nudge, and as I greeted her, I pressed the money into her hand. It was God's gift of encouragement and my joy to be his messenger.

The really important things in life are simple, and the simple things aren't hard to do. Just love people and give what you have in your hand at the time, and God will take that little and make it much! A smile, a prayer, a touch on the arm – all of it is huge in God's economy."

Thank you to the members of Ignite Church for sharing your stories of kindness and proving that oftentimes, the greatest gift comes from being the giver.

A Bus Stop, Braces and a Batch of Cookies

Imagine if you could do one thing today that someone else would remember six decades from now.

It's very possible that something you say or do, either positive or negative, will make such an impact on another person that he or she will remember it for years to come.

Don't believe me? Ask Maxine Jeffries from Underwood, Minn. Here's the letter she sent me:

"Dear Nicole, your articles on the kindness of others brings to mind one angel I had 59 years ago. My oldest son became ill with polio at the age of 6 and was paralyzed from the neck down.

After weeks in the hospital, he started moving parts of his body, but needed therapy at a clinic three times a week. We had to take a bus to the center of town and cross two streets to make it to the clinic. My 4-year-old had to hang on my shirttail as we crossed those streets, because I had to carry his 6-year-old brother, braces and all, and that took both arms.

A policeman saw us one day, got our schedule and was there to carry my son for me for several weeks of therapy. On our very last trip, I made him a batch of cookies, but I know that could never repay him.

Even at 84 years of age, I've never forgotten his kindness. That police officer is just one of hundreds of kind people we have met over the years.

My son wasn't supposed to live past the age of 25. He's now 65. He and his brother live together and are still as close as when they were little – still looking out for each other."

Maxine, I am overwhelmed by the beauty in your story, the

kindness you have shown your little boys, the kindness they now show each other, and the fact that after almost 60 years, you still remember the gestures of one very kind police officer.

Charlie's Story

School is out for the summer in Fargo, so I feel it's safe to let you in on a little family drama. My sweet, 6-year-old boy, Charlie, made a really bad decision a few weeks ago.

Before you accuse me of throwing him under the bus, believe me, I am only sharing this because the entire family learned a lot about kindness from this experience.

Charlie was sitting in his kindergarten classroom looking at his nails that desperately needed to be cut (mom's fault). Two of his classmates dared him to see what would happen if he dragged those sharp little nails across the arm of another unsuspecting boy.

Guess what? Sharp nails on skin cause blood. Not a pretty picture. Charlie felt awful and so did I when I got the email from his teacher explaining what had happened.

I literally cried when I read the email. I cried again when I talked to the teacher on the phone. Then I cried some more when Charlie got home and explained what had happened in his own words.

I just kept thinking, *"Is this it? Is this the moment I will always remember as The Day My Good Son Went Bad? How could I not have seen this coming? Will Social Services take all of my children away because of my inadequate parenting skills?"*

Was I overreacting? Yes, but I was in a pretty low place.

I eventually pulled myself together and tried to work out a solution with Charlie. We decided that he should take his own money and buy some candy for the boy as a form of apology.

Charlie hung his head as we walked into the store. I could see in his eyes how little self worth he was carrying around. My heart hurt for him, but I couldn't quite find the words to tell him that he was a great kid even though he didn't make a great decision.

It turns out I didn't have to.

My idea was to buy a sucker and some gum for the injured party. Charlie's idea was to fill a bag with everything else in the candy aisle. As we looked at all the options, Charlie got more and more excited. He kept saying, *"Mom, Cole will LOVE this!"*

By the time we left the store, Charlie was glowing. He was so excited to deliver the gift to his friend.

It turns out, giving Charlie the opportunity to be kind allowed him to rebuild his self worth. He started to see himself again as a person who is smart, honest and kind.

And as I always say, kindness comes back to you.

Cole's dad sent me this email a few days later:

"Hi Nicole,

That was awfully nice of you and Charlie to drop off that package for Cole. He was pretty excited. Thank you! What a sweet card from Charlie. Don't worry at all about the scratching – not a big deal, 5- and 6-year-olds are really good at doing strange things sometimes.

"Charlie is a super nice kid – I've been in the classroom four or five times now for Junior Achievement, and I can tell you that he is always very well-behaved and attentive – easily one of the best-behaved in the class. I'm sure you have heard the same from the teacher. He always raises his hand if he

wants to say something, waits his turn, and never blurts out.

"Anyway, just thought I'd drop you a line since we all have a tendency to worry too much about what our kids do sometimes, and it's always nice to get some positive feedback."

Cole's dad could have let the whole situation go. He didn't need to follow up with an email, but I'm sure glad he did. That message means so much to me, because between the lines I got to hear that I'm doing a good job as a mom, and those are some of the kindest words ever.

Easing a Stranger's Stress

My first job was as a television traffic and news reporter for a morning show in Milwaukee.

It was 1998, and I was making $18,000 a year. When the job was offered to me, I was ecstatic. I got to be on TV and they were going to PAY ME!?

I quickly realized that when you're on TV, people tend to think you're wealthy. I was embarrassed by the fact that I had to wear the same three suits over and over again because I couldn't afford anything new. I was constantly explaining that I was "trying out a new hairstyle," when in reality, I just couldn't afford to get it cut.

I loved those years of being young and single and learning how to get by on my own. I'm so thankful for what they taught me about what really matters in life and what's just icing on the cake.

I'm grateful to now be in a position where I can sometimes help others with my time or money. And I'm in awe of other people who make it part of their life's mission, like the man who helped out a young couple when they were down on their luck.

"My name is Nick. My wife, Mandy, had something amazing happen, and I felt the need to share it.

"My wife was in getting an oil change when she was told her vehicle had some additional work that was required. It was not a lot more, a couple hundred dollars, but at the time, it was a lot of money for us.

"She was in the small shop with our two children and Mandy called me with the news, asking, 'Nick, what should I do? What are we going to do?'

"My response was 'Well, I guess you will just have to get it done. We will figure something out.' Mandy became upset over the phone, and you could tell that we were really struggling with having to have the work completed.

"A man had been standing in the shop while she was talking with me. He paid for the work on his car and left.

"Mandy had gone outside for a bit to get some fresh air, and when she got back, the work had been completed. Mandy asked 'What was the total?' as she was going through her purse trying to find her debit card.

"The clerk said, 'Do you remember that man who was in here?' The clerk smiled and said 'Well, he called back and said that he wanted to take care of that nice woman's bill.'

"A man who was a complete stranger, who was seeking nothing more than the opportunity to make someone's day, did so in a big way. It turned a very stressful time into a story we will never forget."

Hale Brings A Ray of Sunshine

Some people just ooze sunshine and enthusiasm wherever they go. You can't help but like them, because their attitude is just contagious.

I've had the chance to spend some time this summer with someone like that. His name is Hale and he is 9 years old.

Hale was in a summer theater program with my kids. Since we have to drive right by his house to get to the theater, I told his mom we would pick him up every day. She thought I was doing her a big favor, but the truth is, I was getting the better end of the deal.

You see, each morning for four weeks, I would gather my three children in the car. They would immediately tune into the DVD player after which all hope of conversation was lost. Then we would stop at Hale's house.

The minute that little boy got in the car, the entire focus changed. The TV went off because we all wanted to hear about Hale's latest adventure at the lake where some critter or another escaped its un-natural habitat or his recent trip to a zoo in Michigan where he learned lions with big manes attract females with a Justin Beiber-like attraction. Hale is a master storyteller.

It didn't take long before Hale wanted to know what he needed to do to get in my kindness column. I told him it was really simple. He just had to tell me about an act of kindness that he had been a part of or seen someone else do.

The next day, I got this story from Hale who talked his older cousin Morgan into writing it.

"Hello, my name is Morgan and here is a story about how my cousin Hale and I helped an injured boy. We were at the

Fargo all-city track meet because our brothers were doing events. Hale and I had been playing in the sandpit area.

"The sandpit was fun-filled and exciting, but then, all of a sudden, a boy swinging on a single monkey bar fell off with a thud. We could hear a quiet sob. Hale and I approached the hurt boy. The kid's wrist looked painful and fractured. Hale told the boy, 'Stay here while we go get help.' Hale and I sprinted up the bleachers to tell my dad about the boy. My dad followed us down the stairs and went to the boy with the fractured wrist.

"While he assessed the situation and walked the boy to an empty picnic table, I ran out onto the track looking for help but did not find any. Hale had more luck. Running along the fence, he spotted a member of the National Guard who agreed to help him. The member of the National Guard called 911 when he saw the boy's wrist. The boy had to keep his arm near his stomach and not move it until the ambulance came and took him to the hospital."

I can just picture those two kids running as fast as their legs would take them to help save the day.

I asked Hale why this story of kindness was important to him. He told me it made him feel so good to be able to help someone else, and that every time he thinks about it, he still gets that happy feeling.

Being kind isn't a five-minute high. It's a feeling that refreshes itself each time you revisit that experience in your mind. It can pick you up when you're feeling tired, emotional or unsure of yourself.

Thanks, Morgan, for helping your cousin write that great story. And thanks, Hale, for bringing so much sunshine to our summer.

Ralph's Ride

There is a quote I recently heard that seems to be sticking in my brain. Mother Angelica said, "Unless we dare to accomplish the ridiculous, God cannot accomplish the miraculous."

I don't know if you believe in God or not, and frankly, for the purpose of this column it doesn't matter. What that quote says to me is this: Unless you are willing to take a risk, go out on a limb and allow people to think you're crazy, you will never open yourself to experiencing something really amazing.

I got to see something really amazing happen this summer, and it was all because one man and his wife had a crazy idea.

Ralph Jose has been riding motorcycles since he was 16. He's probably nearing 70, although he looks like he's 45 (you're welcome, Ralph). He works at the Fercho Branch YMCA in downtown Fargo, and as the Y puts it on its website:

"When he married Darlene 50 years ago, it was no question that cycling was going to be a part of their lives. It was something they truly enjoyed doing together. Ralph and his wife have been touring the U.S., Canada and even Europe, and now have one state left to go to – Alaska! So to celebrate their 50th state and their 50th anniversary, they decided to take the trip!"

Here's where some of the "ridiculous" comes in. Those two crazy love birds decided to ride their motorcycle nearly 8,000 miles to Alaska and back. You might imagine an open road, beautiful sky and secret discoveries along the way, but over that long of a journey, road maps, rainstorms and a vibrating butt are also the reality.

But here's where the "miraculous" comes in. Ralph and

Darlene decided to celebrate their trip, their 50th state and their 50 years of marriage by inviting people to celebrate with them.

Ralph put a little table in the fitness center with a sign-up sheet. No pressure, the sign simply said if you want to make a donation to help celebrate the trip, Ralph and his wife would give the money to help kids in need attend Y programs.

Within days Ralph had three sheets filled with people pledging to give $25, $50, $100 and more. Dakota Medical Foundation offered to match those donations up to $2,500. In all, more than 100 people donated to Ralph's Ride, totaling more than $7,000. That's $7,000 not being used for gas, meals or lodging, but simply to give kids a chance to play Y basketball, get a membership for a whole year or go to camp.

"The stars are lining up perfectly for us," Ralph explained. "We have been planning this trip for years."

"I love children," Ralph continued. "And all of the money derived from this trip (through pledges) will go straight to the Partner of Youth Campaign."

Ralph and Darlene left on their big trip June 30th and got home July 31st. Ralph says he and Darlene were in awe of the kindness of people. They never imagined how full their hearts would be with the joy that comes from bringing people together to help others.

Welcome home, Ralph and Darlene, and congratulations! A ridiculously miraculous idea sounds like the perfect way to celebrate 50 years of love.

"When you
help others,
you help
yourself."

Learning to Give More at Walmart

I've found myself wondering lately if a little bit of kindness is enough kindness. If you give someone a little piece of you, but you still have much more to give, does that little piece still count as kindness? Let me explain.

I was walking through the cereal aisle at Walmart the other day when a woman stopped me. She had a cart half-filled with food and half-filled with a sleeping infant in a car seat. In broken English, she asked, "Can you help me? I'm very dizzy."

I was alarmed and immediately started asking if she needed to sit down or perhaps needed medical attention, as I was ready to scream my head off for the nearest Walmart employee.

"No." She shook her head. Then she handed me a stack of paper checks. They were WIC (Women, Infants and Children) vouchers to buy food. Food stamps have changed over the years, but in sort of a hazy way, I recognized them. I remember using them when I was a child.

The woman was clearly overwhelmed coordinating the writing on the checks with the food on the shelves. For instance, she had one check for a 32-ounce box of cereal. None of the boxes she could find were that size. Did that mean she could get two smaller boxes? And which boxes qualified?

I couldn't help her answer the question about the size of the box, but I was able to steer her toward the bright orange stickers next to the prices which signified the types of cereal that were WIC approved. I was shocked by how few there were.

She stopped then and looked at me. "Do you have kids?" she

asked.

"Yes, I have three. OK, what else do you need?"

She handed me a paper check for beans. I walked her to another aisle and started doing a mental time check, wondering if I would be able to finish my own shopping and get home in time to pick up my kids from school.

After finding the woman four cans of beans, I figured I'd done my job and was ready to set her free. I handed the last check back to her. It was for $10 worth of produce. I pointed vaguely to another part of the store and said "Produce means fruits and vegetables. You'll find them over there."

As I watched her walk away, I thought to myself, "How confusing to have to pick out fruits and veggies, weigh everything and then add up all the prices. I'm really grateful I don't have to do that."

Then I told the woman to wait up. I asked if she wanted help picking out the produce, and with an exhale that was audible, she said "Yes. Please."

When we finished weighing the oranges, bananas and mangos, she turned to thank me.

"What is your name?" she asked.

And here's where the kindness got confusing. I told her my name and got so excited to tell her about "the nonprofit foundation for women's health and empowerment that I am the volunteer executive director of blah-blah-blah" (as I pulled out my business card), that I completely forgot to ask her own name.

I didn't ask how she was going to carry a sleeping infant and 10 bags of groceries home. I didn't ask what country she was from or how long she'd been here or whether she missed her former home.

As I reflect on that experience, I realize I was so busy trying to do the right thing by solving this woman's problems that I completely missed what she probably wanted the most from Walmart. She wanted a friend.

I'm telling you this story to urge you to think about something. The next time someone stops to ask you a question or to seek your help, I hope you'll do what I didn't do. I hope you'll ask yourself what that person really needs from you. You may be surprised at how much more you get to give.

Help Amid a Family's Pain

My heart aches when I see tragedy in this world, especially tragedy that could have been avoided. That's how I felt the morning I opened the paper and read about the Deutschers, a young couple, their 1-year-old daughter, and their unborn baby who were killed in an accident with a drunken driver.

There is plenty to be angry, ashamed and confused about in this world.

No act of kindness can erase what has been done. We simply cannot change the past. But here is the beauty: We all have the power to decrease the pain.

We all have the power to help another person learn to smile again by showing them kindness and easing their burden through our words and our actions.

I'd like to share with you a letter that I received from a friend of the Deutscher family.

"I can't call it just an 'act of kindness.' I call it true friendship in the wake of a tragedy: continuing on, as needed, for a grieving family. Katie and Dustin Oster were best friends of Aaron and Allison Deutscher, who were killed when their vehicle was struck head-on by a drunk driver on July 6. They have become a Godsend to Tom and Arlene Deutscher, Aaron's parents.

"Putting Aaron's home up for sale was the last thing Tom and Arlene wanted to do, not because they didn't know it needed to be done, but because of what it was going to take to get it ready to be sold. Their son, Aaron, their daughter-in-law, Allison, and their granddaughter, Brielle, lived in this home. Overwhelmed, inconsolable, heartbroken, and not knowing where to start, Tom and Arlene found the strength to begin going through the home.

"Going through Aaron, Allison and Brielle's belongings was heartbreaking and physically draining. There were so many things that needed to be done in order to get the home ready to be put on the market. With Tom and Arlene not living in the West Fargo area, Katie's kindness was priceless.

"Besides mowing the lawn and taking care of the flower beds and garden, Katie helped Tom and Arlene pack, clean, organize, buy food, run errands and whatever else they needed done, without being asked to do it!

"She was there physically, emotionally and spiritually for this family without question or reservation.

"Dustin was right there beside Katie, when it was time for the hard labor like moving furniture and boxes, touching up paint and staining the deck.

"They even got their family members involved in some of these projects. They took care of the last-minute details that really needed to be done quickly, efficiently and without hesitation.

"Katie is still there for them and will continue to make sure their needs are met, doing all she can for Tom and Arlene when they need her. Something tells me that Katie and Dustin's deep friendship and love for Aaron, Allison and Brielle will keep them close to this family forever.

"Arlene and Tom are truly grateful and appreciative to Katie and Dustin for their kindness that is extraordinary in nature, yet simply true to Katie's and Dustin's nature of giving. This is an immense example of unconditional love, not expecting anything in return."

When there is no act of kindness we can do to make someone's pain go away, there is plenty of opportunity to ease an aching heart.

Day Makers

There is a woman I run into on a regular basis who drives me crazy. She is always happy. I mean always.

She teaches a Zumba exercise class, so for a while I thought maybe she was happy all the time because of all of the endorphins she has streaming through her body.

Then she let me in on her secret. She is the founder of a secret society of people who are extremely wealthy in the areas of joy, happiness, contentment, fulfillment and peace. They call themselves the Day Makers.

A Day Maker makes a conscious effort everyday to create interactions with people that will change that person's day in a positive way. Instead of the innate "What's in it for me? How does this affect me?" attitude, Day Makers focus and think about how they physically, emotionally or spiritually can change the other person's day.

Here are the key principles:

- Focus on using talents, gifts and possessions to meet another person's needs.

- Plan detailed praise and deliver it.

- Take the time to listen to people, look them in the eye and absorb their thoughts.

- Communicate openly and honestly.

- Ask people what makes them feel good, and do those things regularly for them.

- Forgive quickly.

- Love people recklessly by putting reason, fear of

getting hurt and justification aside.

- Perhaps most importantly, flip the switch from thinking "me, me, me" to thinking "you, you, you."

There seem to be more people in this Day Maker society than we might realize.

Like the person who made Betty and Jan's day:

"About a month ago my mom and I went to Perkins in Fargo for something to eat. We had a great breakfast. My mom couldn't finish her muffin, so when our waitress came by, I asked her for a box. At the same time I asked for our bill, and she informed us that it had been taken care of by an anonymous patron.

"My mom and I were both in total shock. I would like to take this opportunity to say 'thanks' to that person or people. As I said, I was so surprised I forgot to tell the waitress to give them our 'thank you,' so hopefully they will see this message. It was a delightful treat."

Here are a few more people who fall into the Day Maker category:

"I am an 86-year-old woman who recently decided I really needed to go to the grocery store. When I came out with my loaded cart, a lady helped me put it in my van, complimented me on my outfit and put the cart away for me.

"When I got home to my senior living apartment, a man helped me unload the groceries. He put them in a cart by the elevator while I put my car away.

"Later that afternoon, one of my neighbors gave me a beautiful item she had sewn. These are the kind of acts that prove we indeed have wonderful people in the

Fargo-Moorhead area."

Keep an eye out for people who are unusually happy. You may be lucky enough to have a Day Maker in your presence.

The Privilege of Having a Voice

I've been thinking it's about time to retire this kindness column. I've been feeling busy lately. Really busy.

Diva Connection is taking off (thank you, God), and that means more meetings, more trouble shooting, and more time making sure women in our community who need something connect with the women who can help them.

I started thinking that something in my life has to go. I need to unload some responsibilities, create more hours in the day and become a better planner. I can only do two out of those three things, so I figured after a year of writing about kindness, it may be time to let it go. People either get the fact that being kind feels good and changes our world or they don't. Perhaps there is nothing else I can say about it. Perhaps there are no more stories to share.

Then something happened.

I had the opportunity this week to meet a woman who has fallen on really tough times. About a month ago, she and her fiancé moved to this area from Texas. They planned on living with a friend in North Dakota until they could find their own place.

According to this woman, her fiancé didn't tell her the whole story. He was having an online affair with her friend and wanted to meet his new love interest in person. Long story short, the young woman I met ended up being heart-broken, penniless and desperate to go home.

She just needed to find someone who could afford to buy her a bus ticket back to Texas.

I am blessed. I have a family and friends who would walk through fire to help me in a desperate time. I have come to realize that not everyone is as lucky.

So, I bought the woman a bus ticket.

The problem was I needed to tell my husband that I had just spent a substantial chunk of money on someone we don't even know.

My husband often says he adores the "glory and splendor that is the mystery of his wife." He wasn't thrilled that I had made the decision to spend our money the way I did, but he understood that sometimes he just doesn't understand me. He gave me a big hug and suggested I put together a budget for giving.

I believe people should give others their time, talent and treasure. I volunteer three days a week as the executive director of Diva Connection Foundation. According to my husband, I give financially until it hurts. So what's left? My talent.

When I reflected this week on my experience with that woman from Texas, I realized that I have to keep writing this kindness column as long as The Forum will let me. It is a privilege to have a voice for something. And I believe that my voice was created to remind people that kindness can change this world.

So, there will still be 24 hours in my day, just like in yours. I will still be busy and overwhelmed at times. But when I lay in bed at night, maybe I can rest easy knowing that my 24 hours were well spent. I hope yours are too.

Great Grandma's Tradition

Let the madness begin. Stuffed bellies, ringing bells, gifts to buy, cards to address, long lines, short tempers: Welcome to Thanksgiving Weekend.

Even though many of us will spend this weekend with the people we love the most, it's often as much a time of stress as it is a time of celebration. We know this weekend marks the starting line for the sprint to "get it all done" before Christmas.

It can be hard to turn off the noise and block out the to-do lists enough to remember that Thanksgiving is about giving thanks.

I give thanks for my little people and for the sticky handprints they leave on the furniture, because someday the handprints will be gone and my little people will be big people.

I give thanks for my husband and for the knowledge that the basketball season will eventually end and I'll get to see him again, but in the meantime, he gets to do what he loves for a living.

I give thanks for our health and for the ability we have to pay for an exam when we don't feel well.

I give thanks for my friends and the fact that I can call them at any time and tell them all the things I'm not thankful for.

I give thanks for the love that fills my home because it is always bigger than the biggest tantrum any one of us could throw.

So how do I keep those things in mind during the next four weeks when the cycle of buy-give-get begins to spin out of control?

I'm always looking for ideas. That's why I was thankful for this letter, sent by a woman named Judith, who uses Thanksgiving as a way to make Christmas more about having a meaningful experience and less about materialism.

"Dear Nicole,

At the risk of sounding 'prideful,' I want to share how I have been trying in some small way to forward good deeds and kindness within my family.

Quite a few years back, I started a tradition that has multiplied and blessed our Christmas celebration.

I give each of my children's families a check at Thanksgiving. I am blessed with four children who each have families of their own. There are 13 grandchildren, and now I am also a great-grandmother of five.

The check is for each family to spend to help a person, group or organization. The money is in place of what I would have spent on gifts for the children and grandchildren. Their gift to me is to share with everyone when we gather on Christmas day how they used their money.

The different choices, the reasons for the choices, the sharing with each other, it just could not be any better than that. I do still buy gifts for the younger grandchildren, but once a grandchild graduates from high school, they are part of the Thanksgiving 'give back' gift.

It has been such a joy to see how they have embraced the idea and how the younger children get excited about the process and want to be involved. I think if this tradition of ours is helping to plant the seeds in these young people, it can't help but grow a garden of goodness that will continue for a long time."

Thanks, Judith. What a wonderful way to turn the next four weeks into a time to focus on the needs of others instead of on what we think needs to be done.

It may be worth mentioning that Judith is a widow who is living on a fixed income. As she says, "It certainly does not require great riches to have enough to share."

Simplify Your Life

How are those New Year's Resolutions coming?

Every year, I resolve not to make a resolution. I find the New Year is a good time to sit back and give myself credit for the things I'm doing right instead of trying to fix all of my "problem areas."

It's kind of like a little gift I give to myself, "Hey Nicole, you're doing a pretty good job of being you. Keep it up!"

This year, my whole plan got derailed thanks to my pesky sister-in-law. This Christmas she decided to shake things up a little bit. Instead of getting me some totally adorable notecards or a sarcastic plaque for my home that reads "Remember, as far as everyone knows we are a nice, normal family," my sister-in-law got me a book.

The nerve, right?

In my hectic world of being a mom, wife and writer, she actually expects me to read?

The book is called "100 Ways to Simplify Your Life." It's written by a Christian author and speaker named Joyce Meyer.

I've read other books by Joyce Meyer, and I especially love listening to her podcasts because I can do that at the gym while I'm running on the track.

So here we are a few days into January, and I've decided to make not one resolution, not two resolutions, but 100 resolutions.

I am clearly an all-or-nothing sort of person.

I opened the book with the great intention of knocking out

one resolution a day. That means in 100 days, by April 10, I would have them all done and could go back to telling myself how great I am.

The problem is that these resolutions are hard. At least the first one is. I'm still stuck on No. 1: Do one thing at a time.

It sounds easy enough, until you really stop to think about how many things you do at once. For instance, I mentioned that I like to get my spiritual guidance from listening to podcasts while running at the gym. Did I mention I also like to check my email and return text messages at the gym?

Just last week, I scheduled a baby shower while I was there, too.

Those are all important things in my life, but perhaps they would all get done less frantically and with more excellence if I did them one at a time.

The biggest thing I've learned about trying to do one thing at a time is that it provides so many more opportunities for kindness.

Returning phone calls while running my kids from school to swimming lessons doesn't leave much time to ask my daughter about her day or find out if my son got to use the tire swing at recess.

When I'm not checking out at the grocery store with a phone to my ear, I can actually hear the clerk when she says my kids are cute. I can sincerely smile at the woman who just held the door for me, and I can return those small favors to others.

I have found more joy and energy in my life by simply focusing on the task at hand. I still have to remind myself many times a day to do just one thing at a time, but it's getting easier, and at the end of the day, I feel a sense of accomplishment instead of feeling drained and exhausted.

I'll have to send my sister-in-law a thank-you note. But not while I'm at the gym.

Kindness in the Shape of a Doughnut

I'd like to explain how Saturday mornings work in the Phillips household.

At about 6 a.m., my almost 3-year-old son, Ben, wakes up, sneaks out of bed and goes to find the dog in her kennel. The dog then wakes up, sees my 8-year-old daughter sleeping and proceeds to jump all over her bed. My daughter, being awakened quite obnoxiously, begins to scream. This immediately acts as an alarm clock with no snooze button, forcing my husband and I to leap out of bed and find out who has been the victim of some hideous crime. Meanwhile, my 7-year-old son is ignoring all the chaos and continues playing on the iPad like he's been doing for the past hour.

To reset the day and bring smiles back to all members of Team Phillips, we do an early morning doughnut run to Hornbacher's. We get some doughnuts, maybe something for dinner if I'm thinking that far in advance, and then go home and settle in. It's really a beautiful thing.

We've been doing this "Phillips Family Saturday Morning Doughnuts" ritual for so long that I don't even feel embarrassed anymore when the employees, like Theresa, Gail, Kelsey and that lovely lady in the bakery department see me in my pajamas. Most times, my mechanic, John, is there, too, and even he has gotten used to seeing my pajama-clad crew walk through the store.

A few weeks ago, little Benjamin and I went to the grocery store for our Saturday morning doughnuts. We said hello to John (apparently he has a Saturday morning grocery store ritual, too), gave Kelsey a hug and meandered back to the bakery.

When we couldn't find the perfect vanilla-frosted cinnamon-flavored as-big-as-your-head doughnut, our favorite bakery lady went to check behind the scenes. Sure enough, she came back with a winner.

I was feeling particularly sharp that morning, so I remembered to grab a bag of frozen ravioli for dinner and then headed to say hello to Gail at the checkout. She smiled, pointed to the next register and said, "Theresa will check you out today."

Theresa rang up the doughnuts and dinner and then said, "You're all set! Someone wanted to pay your bill today." I was dumbfounded. I'm not even sure what I said, I was so shocked. All I remember is that I started to leak from my eyes and hoped like crazy it wouldn't turn into a full-out downpour. Theresa, Gail and Kelsey all just stood there and smiled. I begged them to tell me who had slipped them the money, but they wouldn't budge.

As I drove home, something occurred to me for the first time. Acts of kindness aren't necessarily about doing things for people that they cannot do for themselves. Yes, I could have paid for my groceries. Just like the other snowy morning when I woke up and found that someone had shoveled my sidewalk. I had planned on paying for my groceries. I had planned on shoveling the sidewalk. But it made me feel incredibly special that someone cared enough about me that they would go out of their way to add a sparkle to my day.

Being part of an act of kindness feels like being part of a little miracle. I've heard you can't find them in stores, but apparently, sometimes you can.

We are the Light

"If the darkest hour comes before the light, where is the light? Where is the light? Where is the light?"

Those words are from the song "Ave Mary A" by P!nk. I've listened to that song for years, and yet this week, I felt like I heard it for the first time.

I was thinking about the community of West Fargo, N.D. and how many hearts are breaking at the recent deaths of five students in five separate incidents over a seven-week period. I was thinking about the residents of Newtown, Conn., and how the halls of Sandy Hook Elementary will forever seem haunted by one evil act. I was thinking about the sex trafficking and molestation in America of girls my daughter's age. I was thinking about the amount of people right here in our town who are working so hard to make ends meet and yet have to worry about how they will feed their kids because they don't qualify for assistance.

I was wondering how much darker things need to get before we see the light. And then I realized something. We are the light.

Every time we smile at a stranger, pause a moment longer to hold the door for someone, or just prefer someone's needs over our own, we add light to this world.

NBC News Correspondent Ann Curry started a movement that's gone viral. In response to the shooting deaths in Connecticut, Curry suggested that we honor the lives of those lost by committing 26 acts of kindness. People all over the country are joining in and posting their points of light on Twitter and Facebook.

In its own way, the movement has made it here, too. A Fargo woman and her two children were at West Acres Shopping

Mall on Christmas Eve when an elderly man wearing an oxygen tube slowly walked over and handed her $130. He said he wanted to bless some children in honor of the Sandy Hook students. The woman he gave the money to happened to be a kindergarten teacher. She gave the money to her school counselors who used it to buy milk for kids who couldn't afford a drink at snack time. We are the light.

A single mom sent out a desperate plea on WomensImpact.org for help making her car payments. She was on the brink of losing her vehicle and, without transportation, her three jobs. A stranger, who had once had to flee an abusive relationship and become a single mom, too, offered to help. We are the light.

An assistant coach for the North Dakota State men's basketball team was in Brookings, S.D., for last weekend's game when he found out his little girl was in a Fargo emergency room. An assistant for South Dakota State gave him his car so he could hurry home. We are the light.

A local boy read a story in The Forum about the woman who spent her 25th birthday doing 25 random acts of kindness. He thought it was such a great idea that he celebrated turning 13 by committing his own 13 acts of kindness. His mom took the day off of work to help him. We are the light.

My heart hurts over the pain of this world so much sometimes that it feels like I can't breathe. And then I remember that we are the light.

If you find yourself frustrated over other people's behavior or evilness that seems out of your control, I encourage you to fight back. Take away the darkness by becoming the light.

"Isn't it my job
to keep the light going,
especially
in the dark?"

Hotdish Club

There is an incredible movement of kindness happening at Fargo's Ben Franklin Middle School. I don't know the exact process of the evolution, but it seems to go something like this.

First, there was a principal named John Nelson who reminded the students every day of his personal philosophy: The school is a family, and everyone who sets foot in the building needs to look out for each other.

Then, little kindnesses began to happen, like when the teachers brought new sweatshirts or socks for students who were going without.

Now, the entire Ben Franklin community is coming together in a major way to make sure that the kindness felt on school grounds follows the students home.

It's called the Hot Dish Club.

Last spring, two teachers overheard students talking about how they don't get warm meals at night in their homes. These teachers, Deb Hallquist and Katie Love, felt so strongly about providing for their students that they decided to take action. They pooled their time and money to start the Hot Dish Club.

Deb and Katie sent out a survey to every student in the building to find out who needed a meal and who wanted to volunteer. About 15 students admitted they needed the food and another dozen committed to helping.

Now, every other Tuesday after school, you can find a group of students finding common ground over a hotdish recipe. When they're done measuring and mixing, they take their aluminum pans onto a bus waiting to take them home. The students bake their dinner in their own kitchens so the whole family can enjoy the aroma and the taste of a home-cooked meal.

Deb and Katie still run the program, but they no longer have to foot the entire bill. After sending out an email to their fellow staff members, contributions exploded. Their peers wanted to help and so did many others. Sam's Club gives a monthly gift card, a Bell State Bank & Trust employee gave his Pay it Forward money, parents drop off grocery store cards, a Secret Santa delivered $250, a Girl Scout troop collected a pantry full of food, and many Ben Franklin students even donate their allowances.

A group of Fargo North students heard about the program and made chili so the kids would have a warm meal over the long Christmas break.

Several North Dakota State University students have started stopping by Ben Franklin on Hot Dish Tuesdays to help put together the meals.

Deb and Katie say they love hearing the reactions of their Hot Dish Club members when they report back to school the next day. The kids are proud that they learned how to create a meal and provide for their families.

When I asked the teachers what they wanted from the community, both Deb and Katie said they wanted to make sure you knew that this seemingly large act of kindness is quite simple and could easily be duplicated in other schools, churches and senior centers. They hope the Hot Dish Club becomes contagious, because in their experience, kindness is a dish best served hot.

The Ultimate Act of Kindness

What would you die for? Is there anything or anyone on this earth that is *that* important to you?

I can go through a laundry list of things I'm grateful for, but when it comes down to the nitty-gritty, there are three people for whom I would give my life.

I would die for my children. I truly feel that way. I think most of us as parents do. We cannot stand the thought of losing our children or even seeing them hurting.

That's what gets me about the story of Easter. God loved us so much that He allowed His only son to endure torture and then death so that we could have life in heaven.

I was never able to comprehend the reasoning behind that until I realized that God sees all of us as His children. He knew He had to let one of his children suffer for the benefit of all of them.

It was the ultimate act of kindness.

Easter is the most important holiday on the religious calendar for Christians because it marks our ability to join God in heaven. It is a time of celebration because through His death and resurrection, Jesus paid the price for every sin we will ever commit. God can once again see us as He made us, as perfect creatures.

There is great joy waiting for us every day if we can wake up each morning and look at ourselves through God's eyes. He is not seeing a work in progress, He is seeing a work of art. Knowing that allows us to take risks, like loving others in big ways without the worry of being rejected.

If I could give you one gift today to celebrate the miracle of Easter, I wouldn't give you a basket full of jelly beans or a big chocolate bunny. I would give you this message with the hope that it will remind you to be kinder to yourself: God loves you. He is proud of you, and He thinks you are perfect.

"So now I am giving you a new commandment: Love each other. Just as I have loved you, you should love each other. Your love for one another will prove to the world that you are my disciples." John 13:34–35 (NLT)

A Bridge of Kindness

Have you ever found yourself in a situation that you know calls for thoughtfulness, but you truly don't know which act of kindness could even make a difference?

Last Saturday, I pulled the bright orange plastic bag off my Forum newspaper to see a headline announcing that a Duluth man had died in a plane crash.

As I was finalizing a grocery list for Easter dinner, another woman somewhere was forced to start making funeral arrangements.

I don't know the man or the family, so this could have been a headline that caused a moment of ache in my heart before I moved on to the next thing.

But I was reminded of how closely we all are connected a few days later, when a friend and I took our dogs for a long walk in Johnson Park. She told me she was friends with the man's mother and would be going to the funeral.

My friend was hurting, and I didn't know what to do.

I find myself in that situation a lot. I have another friend who lives far away from Fargo, but I feel her pain across the miles and struggle with what I can do to help.

This friend has seven gorgeous children, all younger than 13. Her oldest daughter has thyroid cancer, so family vacations have been replaced with several trips a year to the Mayo Clinic.

A few weeks ago, this friend found out her 8-year-old son is going blind. She is frantically searching for a surgeon who can fix his eyes. And now her husband has lost his job.

I just sat there and cried when I found out because I want so badly to help her, but what can I do to offset problems that are so big?

It seems futile, but reading her Caring Bridge site reminded me that sometimes it's not the size of the gesture, it's about letting someone know they are not alone. I want to share with you part of her latest post:

"I was blindsided with a gut punch last week. I was upset and sad and anxious and TIRED... When I was told about my son, I fell down... I couldn't stay upright. It's one of those moments where you only have the energy to breath in and out.

"As a friend was saying how she was praying for us and our family (and as ashamed as I am to admit this), I screamed out 'I can't eat prayer! I can't write P-R-A-Y on a check to Mayo and pay for my daughter's cancer check up.' I wasn't upset with her for praying for my family; she knew what I meant. I was broken down from our circumstances.

"Later, I got a phone call from my daughter's basketball coach's wife. She asked me if I could meet her the next day to get my car fixed up. I was so taken aback, all I could do was giggle and sob. I was shocked that someone who knew us would think to help me; with tires. But there's more, stay with me...

"The next day, I was handed a basket from the families at school. In that basket were love offerings like you wouldn't believe! My sweet and dear girlfriends had rounded the wagons around my family and those people loved all over us. We've been given so many blessings: meals for nearly three weeks, gift cards, movie passes, flowers, phone calls, fixed tires, fixed washer... and while waiting for my washer to be fixed, someone came to me and said she couldn't give me much but wanted to give me 10 dollars in coins so I could go to the laundry and wash clothes! How very sweet

and heart-warming. The fact that people are begging to know exactly how to help us, the fact that my hometown is sending me love notes and love offerings... my childhood friends are letting me know they are loving on me in prayer. Oh, I am so humbled and speechless in thanks... and ashamed I threw my little (OK, maybe not so little) tantrum."

I'm so thankful my friend let me share this with you because it is a testimony to the power of love. We don't have to do everything to help a person who is hurting, we just have to do something. Together, those little acts of kindness add up to something very big.

The Color Blue

Everyone makes the choices they make for a reason.

You work at your job because you either love it or you need to get paid. You commit random acts of kindness because you want to make the world a better place or you hope karma will pay you back.

I write this column for two reasons. One, I have a life mission to prove that kindness really is contagious; and two, I am chasing the ever elusive words to explain how amazing it feels to be kind.

I got to see both of my personal motives play out this week in real life.

You have probably heard about things going viral. If songs, dance crazes and wacky videos of cats playing the piano can inspire people to turn on their computers, why can't stories of kindness inspire people to look beyond themselves and reach out a helping hand?

I believe they can, and thanks to readers who continue to share these stories, like Laurelee Oenick from Fargo, kindness is spreading.

"Dear Nicole,

My mom, Judy, lives in Wisconsin and just loves hearing the 'Fargo Nice' stories from your Kindness is Contagious column.

"In our telephone chats I tell her about your column all the time. She agrees with me that Fargo is a very special place to live and raise children.

"She has apparently decided to bring a little bit of 'Fargo Nice' closer to her home in Wisconsin.

"She told me how she was in line at the grocery store the other day and the man in front of her did not have enough cash to pay for all of his groceries. He was about $7 over, so he put aside a frozen pizza and a few other small items. My mom told the cashier that she would pay for the pizza and the other items.

"The man said, 'Oh, are you buying the pizza now?' She replied, 'No, I'm buying it for you! It's called being Fargo Nice. People in Fargo just do nice things for others all the time. Now you can pass it on by doing something Fargo Nice for someone else. Enjoy your pizza!'

"The man thanked her and got into his truck with a surprised expression on his face. My mom is sure he is going to pass it on."

Laurelee, thank you for helping me accomplish one of my two goals by spreading the message of kindness.

Goal No. 2 played out this week when I got to see what it looks like when someone experiences the high of committing a random act of kindness for the very first time.

My 9-year-old daughter was helping me watch my girlfriend's 3-year-old daughter. When the playdate was over, my daughter asked if we could stop at Target to buy a doll for her young friend. She was just certain this little girl's night would be made if we could also make a quick delivery.

So, at 7:30 at night, my daughter was at my friend's front door with the doll in hand. It may have made that little girl's night, but it made my daughter's entire week.

She couldn't stop talking about the look in little Waverly's eyes when she saw the doll. Or how messed up the doll's hair was going to be because Waverly would probably have to sleep with it every night. Or how Waverly would probably

80

treasure the doll so much that she would pass it down to future generations. Well, maybe not, but you get my point.

My daughter finally "got it." She now knows exactly how exhilarating it feels to step out of her comfort zone and love boldly.

Trying to explain that feeling to someone is like trying to explain what the color blue looks like. You've just got to experience it for yourself.

So, as you face a week full of choices both important and mundane, I hope you will commit to making a conscious decision to better your own life and the lives of others by choosing to be kind. You'll be helping me to further my personal missions, and who knows, maybe karma will get you back.

We Are All Broken

I have been trying really hard to become a better person, but I think I've reached a plateau.

I am now to the point where I can control my actions, but I'm having a hard time controlling my thoughts. For example, I will see trash on the sidewalk and stop and pick it up, because I know if I don't, it will be someone else's burden. It's just the kind thing to do.

Then I will be driving in my car and someone will cut me off, and I will think, "What a jerk! Are they trying to kill someone?" Not a very kind thought. Maybe that person is on the way to the hospital. Maybe that person just got some tragic news and he or she is not thinking clearly. Maybe I'm a terrible driver and annoying everyone around me. I simply do not have both sides of the story when I make snap judgments about people or their actions.

A Fargo friend of mine, Shelle Moran, sends out a daily email with inspiring and thought provoking messages. This week, she sent one that cut straight to my heart, because it reminded me of how far I have to grow. I felt compelled to share it with you.

"I recently attended a Narcotics Anonymous meeting as a supporter of some very, very incredible people in my life. As I cheered on those who have made small goals (even hourly goals for some), and cried with those who are feeling great sorrow for what they have done to themselves and others, I think about the laundry list of addiction that each one of us grapples with.

- Addiction to worry

- Addiction to alcohol

- Addiction to money

- Addiction to control

- Addiction to approval

- Addiction to sex

- Addiction to perfection

- Addiction to drugs

- Addiction to work

- Addiction to food

- Addiction to nicotine

"How easy it is to feel justified in turning our backs on folks who have the 'worst' addictions. The truth is we all have frogs that hide in the scum of our ponds. As Day Makers we first identify our addictions and admit them to others. Then we go out and love recklessly. No addiction is more or less of a 'sin.' We are all broken."

Thanks, Shelle, for allowing me to share your thoughts. I think many of us can relate. Kindness often takes the form of an action toward ourselves or others, but perhaps it needs to start in our heads.

For me, that means purposefully rejecting the thoughts that pop into my head that are based on bias or misunderstanding and only allowing myself to honor thoughts that are based in love.

Love builds compassion, and, sometimes, that is the greatest act of kindness we can give.

Lessons from My Mom

If I could change one thing about myself, I would be a better mom.

I never seem to have quite enough patience to ride the tide of mischief that is inevitable with three children. The laundry and the dishes always seem to call out the loudest just when my kids want to snuggle or tell me a story about their day.

I wake up in the morning and ask God to help me be the mom those beautiful kids deserve, and then I lie in bed at night and ask God to forgive me for falling short yet again.

My spirit would be completely broken if I didn't know beyond a shadow of a doubt that kids turn out okay, not despite their parents' weaknesses but often because of them.

My mom is a kind and brilliant woman. She speaks three languages, is constantly in a state of learning something new, and shares her heart with others through her volunteer work. She is an enviable role-model.

I think my mom is someone I admire so much because she is proof that we can turn our lives around.

When I was in third grade, my mom made a tragic decision. She got a job teaching at a prison and fell in love with an inmate. She lost her husband (my father), her home, her job, and for a while, she lost her kids.

When her new husband was released from prison, he had an affair and the relationship was over. My mother ended up haunted by financial problems, depression and a palpable guilt over what she had done and all she had lost.

It took me a long time to understand that she always loved me. She just couldn't take care of me and herself at the same time.

During all of the conversations we have had about this over the past few decades, one theme keeps popping up. My mom says the attention from this man was like a drug. She needed it. It clouded her vision until she couldn't see how it was destroying her life. When she finally figured it out, it was too late. The damage was done.

Thankfully, the story doesn't end there. Through the sadness and shame, my mom went back to school and earned her master's degree at the age of 50. She ran her first full marathon on her 60th birthday. She bought her first home, all by herself, when she was almost 70.

My mom owns her mistakes. She takes full responsibility for them, but she refuses to let the past determine her future.

Mom, I appreciate you letting me share this story as a way to give hope to other people who are feeling like their sins are too big to be forgiven or that it's too late to begin again.

I love you very much. If you are proud of the woman I've become, please know, it is all because of the woman you have become. Happy Mother's Day. Love, Nicki

Ripples of Kindness

When I started writing this column, I was excited to hear from the people of Fargo-Moorhead.

I had a hunch there were beautiful acts of kindness happening all around me, but I wasn't quite sure how to find them. So, I put out a call for help. I asked readers to send me their stories of kindness, and I prayed. I hoped people would be open enough to share their stories with me and with an entire newspaper audience, and I desperately prayed people would take the time to actually write those stories down and send them in.

I was looking for several things. I wanted to hear about the times when people initiated an act of kindness and how great it made them feel, but I also wanted to hear about those times when kindness had taken them by surprise and touched their hearts on a day when they may have needed it most.

I still get a jolt of joy everytime I open my email or find a letter on my desk addressed, "Kindness is Contagious." I love reading the stories that come straight from the lives of people in the Red River Valley. When they write about something that happened at the mall or the grocery store, it resonates with me, because I've walked down those same aisles. I am reminded on a daily basis, regardless of what the rest of the newspaper says, that goodness exists in my community.

What I never guessed when I asked for those stories is how often I would become part of the circle of kindness and how far the ripples of kindness would reach. Here's what I haven't told you about the mail I've gotten. More often than not, there is money involved.

People have sent me checks to pass along to Samaritan's

Feet, Women's Impact, my friend whose son is losing his vision, the lady who needed money for a bus ticket, and many other causes I have talked about in this column. Several of you have sent checks payable to me, asking me to do an act of kindness on your behalf.

I am honored to be trusted with such a beautiful task, but honestly, I'm also stunned. I simply cannot believe the generosity in your hearts.

A woman in her 90s started writing weekly letters to my children after I mentioned in a column how much I long for local grandparents for my little ones. Now my kids are learning what it was like to take a horse and buggy to a one-room North Dakota schoolhouse, and they are practicing their letter-writing skills.

I have been the recipient of colorful letters myself from the Kindness Club in Evansville, Minn. Barb Bratvold is the teacher who started the club in 1995. Since that time, 316 students have been inducted as lifetime members, sending out more than 47,000 greeting cards to people who are lonely, facing adversity or could just use a smile. My cards came from first and second-graders, and they sure did brighten my day!

But wait, there's more. A man from Kentucky sent me a book, called "Random Acts of Kindness," he thought I might enjoy reading.

A retired letter carrier from Canada who has been nicknamed "The Singing Postie," sent me a stack of his inspirational writing.

I have even gotten a letter from a South Dakota man serving time at the U.S. penitentiary in Kansas. He just wanted to tell me he now knows how important kindness is in this world.

When I started writing this column, I hoped that by sharing essays of kindness, we could convince people in the Fargo-Moorhead area to step out of their comfort zones and show love. I believe that is happening, thanks to your stories. But also, thanks to your stories, the kindness isn't limited by geography. What I have found out from people in Florida, California, Kentucky, Canada and Kansas is that kindness matters all over this world and it really is contagious.

Integrity & Kindness Go Together

I don't remember when I first heard the word "integrity," but I remember hearing it, and for a long time, only having a vague idea of the meaning.

Merriam-Webster has three definitions for Integrity:

*Firm adherence to a code of especially moral or artistic values.

*An unimpaired condition.

*The quality or state of being complete or undivided.

Those definitions seem a bit technical to me. I like to think of integrity as simply doing the right thing, even when nobody is watching.

The sermon in my church recently was all about living a life of integrity, but it took a different approach than I had ever considered. Part of the sermon focused on having integrity in the way you give by giving to those you love, to those who are in need, and to those who have been wronged.

For the first time, I realized that integrity and kindness go hand in hand.

Kindness is sometimes randomly bestowed upon a stranger, but we are most frequently kind to the people we love. That form of kindness seems pretty easy.

Occasionally, someone in need crosses our path, and we show kindness by helping him or her out as best we can. Kindness in these situations can be a little more difficult because people have different ideas about who is "needy."

I feel like kindness becomes really tricky when we're dealing with someone who has been wronged, because that often means we have to stick our noses into situations that may be none of our business. It is in those times, however, that integrity and kindness shine. Take the example sent in by 24-year-old Liz Michels.

"This past week, I went to a restaurant to enjoy a nice lunch, and I saw something that just shocked me.

"Now, first I have to say everyone knows the Golden Rule 'Do Unto Others As You Would Have Them Do Unto You.' We all learned it in elementary school, and it continues with us every day.

"Well, as I was sitting at my table at the restaurant, I noticed a couple giving their waitress a hard time. They were yelling at her, saying she wasn't doing her job right and they demanded to see her manager. The waitress was on the verge of tears, but she kept her composure and got her boss. Luckily, the manager fixed everything, but the worst part was yet to come.

"Before the couple left, they went back to the waitress and yelled at her again and then refused to leave her a tip even though, as far as I could tell, she did nothing wrong.

"As I continued eating my lunch, I saw her working really hard and doing everything she was supposed to be doing. She wasn't my waitress, but I knew I had to do something for her.

"Before I left, I handed her a tip and said how sorry I was that those people were so rude to her. Her face was priceless when I handed her the money. She clearly was not expecting it.

"She thanked me several times and said she was trying to do an honest day's work and that she just wanted to make a living for herself. I knew that giving her that tip was the right thing to do. It made my day knowing that I could make such a difference in another person's day and make someone feel appreciated.

"I wanted to write about this experience because I want to show others that kindness can go a long way in making a difference in this world."

Thank you, Liz, for sharing your story. It's very easy to turn away and pretend we don't see someone being wronged. We can even justify our actions by saying, "It's none of my business." It takes true integrity to instead heal the hurt with kindness.

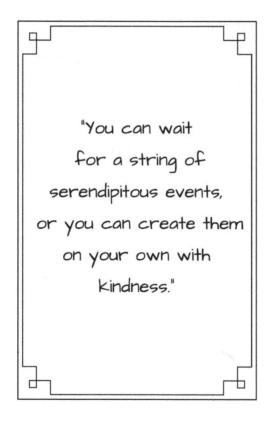

"You can wait
for a string of
serendipitous events,
or you can create them
on your own with
kindness."

Serendipitous Kindness

I love stories of serendipitous kindness.

Those times when someone calls just when you need to talk, a friend delivers a book that contains the exact words you need to hear, or a stranger delivers a compliment at the precise moment you need it most.

This has happened hundreds of times in my life, but one time stands out from the rest. I was buying a sandwich at a deli when the woman behind the counter looked right at me and said, "You have such beautiful eyes."

I have always believed the old proverb that says the eyes are the windows to the soul. Well, my soul was hurting that day, and having a stranger make that comment touched me deeply. I started to cry on the spot, which I'm sure made the woman immediately regret the compliment! As I wiped away the tears, I simply said, "Thank you. I really needed to hear that today."

The magical thing about kindness is that it always hits the mark. We don't know what's happening in someone's life or what they need from us, but God does. It's stunning to see how He uses us to lift up our fellow human beings.

I received the following email from a woman who was very thankful to be the beneficiary of serendipitous kindness:

"Nicole, I would like to share an act of kindness that happened to me at Walmart.

"It was a particularly hard, depressing day for me, because my family is having issues with our son and his wife. We were informed that we will no longer be able to be a part of our granddaughter's life. I have taken care of her quite frequently since she was a baby. She is now 3, and to have her cut out of our lives cold turkey was weighing on my heart and soul.

"I went to Walmart on 52nd Avenue in Fargo to pick up a few things. When I was done shopping and leaving the store, a lady came up to me, handed me a rose and said, 'This is an act of kindness.' I thanked her for the flower, and it hit me that I really did need that rose at that time. It sure lifted my spirits when I needed them lifted. I went to my car and began to cry. I had been fighting back the tears from feeling so down, and this woman and the rose made me feel better right away."

Thank you for sharing your story, Barb. I hope the woman who gave you that flower knows the timing of her act of kindness was anything but random.

Spilled Cereal Isn't So Bad

My son spilled his entire bowl of cereal today.

He was supposed to be sitting at the table eating his breakfast. Instead, like a typical 3-year-old, he was bouncing around in his chair and trying to see if he could balance his spoon on the edge of the bowl. The next thing you know, Lucky Charms are flying through the air.

It was almost enough to send me into the "I told you to sit still!" mom-tirade. Almost. Instead, I thanked God that my little boy is healthy and happy and sitting on my kitchen chair instead of lying in a hospital bed.

Thanks to Michelle Kliem, a concerned grandmother from Carrington, N.D., I remembered to count my blessings. Here is the letter she sent me.

"Tragedy struck our family last week, making it hard to smile. But as I was running my normal three-mile stretch today, I began thinking of all the random acts of kindness others have shown to our family, and I instantly felt blessed. I feel the need to tell our story so everyone knows it's true, that each one of us can make a difference in the life of another.

"On June 11, my 5-year old grandson asked his mom if he could go play with his friends across the street. He lives on a quiet street in West Fargo, not a through street, with nothing behind his house but a man-made pond and fields.

"He jumped on his bike and two seconds later was hit by a vehicle. He went flying through the air, and in his words, into the clouds.

"Shortly thereafter the ambulance came and out jumped the EMT angels. They started asking Teegan his name and kept him talking while they went to work. They made the 'mistake' of cutting off his favorite Bison shirt, which did not go without comment from the broken little boy. The EMTs didn't know that he loves the North Dakota State University Bison, that their Christmas card shows the family in Bison-wear, or that Teegan is pictured with the team's quarterback, Brock Jensen.

"My husband and I jumped in the car and journeyed to Fargo to see our little man. He was so covered with road rash that the only way we knew to love him up was to rub noses with him. He was lying in a hospital bed, broken with fractured collarbones, ribs, a shoulder blade and small holes in both lungs. My heart still bleeds for him.

"One day later, while Teegan was lying in that hospital bed as white as the sheets that covered him, two EMTs showed up to see how he was doing. They brought him new Bison clothes.

"His Uncle Ryan came to visit with a tractor balloon so big one had to walk around it.

"His dad's friend, Mitch, came to visit, himself a father to four young kids, bringing Teegan a digger.

"Last Friday, Teegan got another surprise visit. Brock Jensen and Zach Vraa, two NDSU Bison football players and heroes to Teegan, showed up. What an impact on a broken little boy! Those two college athletes, living their own busy lives, showed up to brighten a long, depressing day for a young child.

"Teegan is getting stronger each day. He stood for the first time but is afraid to walk as the orthopedic surgeon designed a halter for him to wear that binds his arms against his chest. I think he knows if he trips or stumbles he can't catch himself and will only fall and injure his already broken torso.

"His road rash is healing rapidly, and he finally got to go home. You can tell Teegan is starting to feel better because he is now concerned about the welfare of his bike.

"I wanted to write this letter to say, 'Thank you,' to all the people who have taken the time to check in on Teegan and raise his spirits.

"Don't think for a moment you can't make a difference in the lives of others. All it takes is your time."

Lasting Love

I love it when people ask my husband, "Is your wife really as kind as she seems?"

It's a very sweet question, but the real reason I love it is because it always puts my husband on the spot. It's a Catch-22.

If he says, "No" then he looks like a guy who should be writing a Meanness is Contagious column. If he says, "Yes!" then he is a liar.

I'll be honest. My husband gets the worst of me. There are times when I'm preoccupied or just plain tired and expect him to deal with the fact that I don't feel like listening to the trials and tribulations of being a basketball coach.

If I have had a bad day, though, he had better be waiting to hear all about it with a compassionate and attentive ear.

Hell hath no fury like a woman who notices her husband watching SportsCenter while she is trying to complain about something.

There are days when I wouldn't blame him for telling people about my mean streak, and other days when he says I make him a better person. We are in it 'til death do us part, which for us means that we have to look at the long-term rewards of our relationship instead of getting caught up in any minor annoyances.

I was reminded of this principle recently while reading the eulogy my step-mother, Deb, wrote when her mom passed away.

"When Mom first met Dad at age 15, she knew she wanted to marry him. He was 'her Ken' as she always liked to say, as well as the smartest and most handsome man around. When they married, Grandma had Dad promise he always would take care of Mom. After Mom's dementia became advanced, Dad delayed moving Mom to an assisted living facility because of this promise. Also, Dad liked taking care of Mom. He loved washing her hair and helping her in every way he could.

"Dad did the best he could, but it just got too hard, and we persuaded him it was time. Moving Mom to a facility was the most difficult thing he ever did. This, however, also was a way of taking care of Mom. Dad lovingly took care of her for 64 years.

"Even when neither Mom nor Dad could communicate because of her dementia and his stroke, it was clear how they felt about each other. After Mom's dementia diagnosis, Dad showed Mom a lot of physical affection with hugs and back rubs. His patience with her forgetfulness and memory loss was incredible. Although Mom's physical appearance deteriorated, Dad's eyes would light up when he saw Mom as if she were the most beautiful woman alive.

"Every chance he had, he would hold and stroke Mom's hand. He made sure she knew he always would be there for her. It was evident Mom knew Dad and was aware he loved her more than ever."

Thank you, Deb, for letting me share that touching tribute to your mother.

A life well-lived and well-loved is about letting kindness carry you through the ebb and flow of this world, with the one you love.

Good Virus

I've been trying to become a person of purpose. I want to know why I'm doing the things I'm doing.

I take a shower because I went running and I stink. I brush my teeth because I ate garlic and my family is shunning me. I put that cookie in my mouth because I'm hungry. Or I'm bored. Or I'm tired. Or I'm worried.

There are a million little decisions I make and actions I take every day. Some of them I think about, and some I just do because it's what I've always done.

I'm starting to think about all of those little actions. Why do I do what I do? Why do I choose to be kind? It feels good, which is the basic reason, but I keep coming back to the idea that there must be a bigger driving force.

At the same time these thoughts were going through my head, there was a man on his computer in Los Angeles searching the words "Kindness is Contagious." Guess what he found? Me.

I love the way the world works. You see, this man unknowingly gave me exactly what I was looking for: scientific evidence proving it pays to be kind and that kindness truly is contagious.

David Gaz was born in Michigan, grew up in New Jersey, studied in Los Angeles, moved to Paris, then San Francisco and is now back in L.A. Gaz says he's always had a concern with the status quo, but it has been more about critiquing it rather than fixing it. Three years ago, his wife suggested that he focus on the positive, so he began researching kindness.

That research gave birth to a documentary called "Good Virus" in which Gaz combines data from top scientists, historical evidence and social trends in a fascinating 76-minute movie.

The whole thing is narrated by Catherine Ryan Hyde, the best-selling author of the novel and film "Pay It Forward."

She was the woman who introduced the entire world to the idea of organized kindness: Pay a kindness to three people and ask each of them to pay it to three others, and so on, and eventually the kindness will come back to you. It works on multiplication of threes, so even if lots of people drop the ball, the enormity of the exponential system of math keeps the cycle of kindness going.

When Gaz emailed me, asking if I'd like to take a look at his documentary, I thought, "Sure, I'm always interested in things dealing with kindness." Twenty minutes into the movie, I had to start taking notes because there were so many things I wanted to research on my own. I was mesmerized.

Did you know Charles Darwin claimed sympathy is our strongest instinct? Getting our genes passed on to the next generation is so vitally important that our nervous system actually evolved to help us be kind to our offspring. I knew there was a reason I have never had the urge to eat my young.

That's in the movie.

Did you know kind people do better than their less-kind counterparts in competitive life-skills games? People trust them more and give them more resources, so they end up winning.

That's in the movie.

Did you know that people who interacted online with someone who was kind became kind themselves, which in turn affected their other online relationships?

That's in the movie.

I can almost hear you skeptics out there shouting scary scientific words at me like variable, control group and confidence interval.

That's in the movie.

They interview researchers from Harvard and Berkeley who have scientifically proven (with control groups, variables and the whole nine yards) that kindness is contagious and that nice guys finish first.

Kindness matters. It is contagious. And there are plenty of people in this world working to prove it.

When Kindness Takes Some Effort

I get a lot of credit that I simply don't deserve. People approach me at church or the grocery store and say they love reading my column. But the truth is, it's not my column. It's the community's column. If people didn't share their stories of kindness with me, I would have nothing to write.

Sure, I could get by for a few weeks by talking about someone who was especially nice to me at the gas station or something sweet my kids did for another little girl or boy, but very quickly I would run out of stories to tell.

The very thing that breathes life into these words is the very thing I get all the credit for: being kind.

I'm a little ashamed to admit that I am still developing the fruit of kindness in my life.

There are days when I am standing at the kitchen sink feeling sorry for myself for no good reason. When I start examining that self-pity, I quickly realize that I have spent too much time with an inward focus and not enough time looking at the needs of others.

There are days when I fool myself into believing I've got this kindness thing mastered, only to turn around and do something really ugly. I blame my husband for my own lack of planning or I lose my patience with my kids. My ugliness always seems to strike hardest on those I love the most.

In those times, kindness becomes an effort, but it also becomes the key to loving and forgiving myself and breaking free from self-pity. When I turn my gaze outward, I find opportunities to be kind. That kindness leads to gratefulness. That gratefulness extinguishes my selfishness.

On the hardest days, I have to look at kindness almost like

homework. I have to intentionally decide to get back on track.

I am incredibly proud that someone from our little corner of the world is helping the entire nation to do just that. This person, who wishes to remain anonymous, has started a website devoted to deliberate acts of kindness, simply because he or she wants to encourage people to be kind on purpose.

You can buy a wristband or a T-shirt, but the crux of 40AOK.com lies in the cards. There are 40 squares on each card. Each time you complete an act of kindness, you get to mark it off in a square. The creator of the site says, if you need motivation, you can reward yourself after completing each set of 10 squares, but I think you'll find the reward comes every time you make the effort to be kind.

I hope you're not like me. I hope kindness is such a part of your personality that it shines consistently and constantly. But if you sometimes find yourself in need of a little reminder, be kind to yourself. Tell those you have hurt that you are sorry and then remember that perfection isn't the goal. Kindness is.

Love is a Verb

On Monday, my husband and I will celebrate our anniversary. The fact that we've been married for 13 years kind of blows me away.

In my mind, I'm still 28, so that would mean I got married when I was 15. Can you see how the math plays tricks on me?

When I married my husband, I adored him. I was in love with him, but there was also a part of me that was infatuated with him.

Thirteen years later, I am still in love with him, but now instead of infatuation, I feel gratitude. I am grateful for his loyalty, patience and laughter.

I think God knew he needed to pair me with someone who would see the humor in my many idiosyncrasies. As Saul (my husband) often says, "It's just part of the glory and splendor that is the mystery of my wife."

Thirteen years seem to have passed by in an instant, and yet we know they happened because we have three children who still wake us up every morning, reminding us that we are no longer in our 20s.

While 13 seems like a lot of years to us, today is the anniversary of a couple who is celebrating 50 years of marriage. That doesn't happen very often anymore.

Dina and Bill Brady were married Aug. 17, 1963. They had three children and now get to spoil seven grandchildren. It's my understanding they met in Ada, Minn., but have spent the majority of their lives in Fargo.

My friend Sarah (Dina and Bill's daughter-in-law), asked if I would write a short congratulatory note to her in-laws. As I reflected on marriage and tried to find just the right words, I realized that the task of summing up 50 years is impossible.

No one except the couple involved knows how many trials were faced and how many obstacles were overcome.

I am certain that in 50 years of marriage, there have been disagreements over how money should be spent or how children should be raised. I am certain there were times when faithfulness, patience and self-control were tested.

To say, "Congratulations" to those of you who have made the decision to stay married through thick and thin, through good times and bad, through sickness and in health seems inadequate.

Taking a vow and then fulfilling it has allowed the Bradys' children to see how two people work together to keep a family intact. That's a big deal.

I wasn't raised in a home where Mom and Dad shared the same address. I looked to the parents of my friends for examples of how a husband and wife are supposed to interact.

Now, being married myself, I can finally see how the bond between a husband and wife changes, some days cracking and weakening and other days growing stronger than ever.

Dina and Bill have given their children a great gift. They have taught their children that love is not a feeling; it's an action. That is a lesson in kindness that takes a lifetime to teach.

Saying Goodbye to Robby Dog

I recently received an email that immediately took my heart back to this time last year. School had just started, and my family was all caught up in the fun of anticipating a season of changes.

One of the changes we hadn't anticipated was the loss of the smallest, furriest member of our family. Robby Dog was a 12-year-old Shih Tzu; a fluffy, tan ball who in his younger days was playful and patient, but in his later years got a little crabby when the kids tried to hug him.

I came home from work one day to find that Robby Dog had a scratch on his eye. It looked awfully painful so we took him to the vet. My husband and I never expected to hear her diagnosis: the eye would have to be removed. We also didn't expect her next observation: Robby Dog could only see shadows out of the other eye. Removing the injured eye would mean that he would be almost totally blind.

While the veterinarian explained that dogs are resilient and can learn to live without sight, she kindly explained that we really needed to consider all of our dog's health issues. She said it may be time to say goodbye.

Saul and I struggled with that news. We felt very torn knowing there was something that could medically be done but that we had the option to take another path.

Eventually, we came to the conclusion that our time with Robby Dog had to come to an end. It was heart-breaking. I sobbed. Tears are running down my cheeks even now as I write this, remembering how very sad it was to hold him for the last time.

Normally in this type of circumstance, I would call my friends and they would have the perfect words to soothe my soul. Unfortunately, this time when I thought of picking up the phone, I couldn't do it. Some little voice deep inside me whispered, "It's just a dog. It wasn't a child. Get over it."

Getting over it was harder than I expected. Robby Dog wasn't just an animal. He was a walking reminder of many tender moments in my life. He joined our family right after Saul and I got married. He met my newborn daughter at the door when I brought her home from the hospital. He snuggled right next to me as we drove to Fargo for the first time. He helped me explore our new neighborhood before I had any friends to join me.

Losing him felt like losing a segment of my life. I didn't think there was anyone I could talk to who would understand that feeling.

The email I got recently from Amanda Thornton reminded me of that time. That's why when she asked if I would help her thank a stranger for an act of kindness, I couldn't refuse Amanda's request:

"My husband and I would like to thank someone who did something very compassionate and generous for us during a difficult time. We thought this column might reach her.

"On June 1 my husband and I had to put our cat, Smokie, to sleep at the FM Animal Hospital in Moorhead. It was a very tough decision, but she had been sick for a long time and was suffering.

"Before the procedure, we paid for her to be buried in the pet cemetery. It was $110, and we had to pay in cash. We paid the money and then went back with Smokie. We stayed with her until she was gone, petting her and saying goodbye.

"Before we left, one of the receptionists came in and told us that a woman had paid for Smokie's burial costs and handed us our money back. It was such a kind gesture, and we've wanted to offer our thanks ever since."

Someone in that clinic knew Amanda's pain and reached out in a very tangible way to show the Thorntons they weren't alone. Hearing that story helps me understand that I wasn't alone in my grief either. Thanks to the love of a stranger, we are all able to apply the soothing balm of kindness.

The One Who Gives is the One Who Gets

When I worked on TV, my husband always said I considered it a job well done if I could make people at home laugh while I was delivering the news.

Now that I write for the paper, he is accusing me of trying to make people cry.

The other day, I wrote a story about the time we had to put down our beloved Robby Dog. It tied in with a letter I got from Amanda Thornton about how a stranger at the veterinary clinic paid for her cat's passing. Amanda was hoping to say "thank you" to the person who so deeply touched her heart.

Part of my family's Saturday morning tradition (other than going to the grocery store for donuts) is to read my column.

Well, there I was, sitting on the couch with all of "Team Phillips," reading about Robby Dog and Amanda's cat. I had written the column, so I thought I was immune to what was in it, but when my daughter's eyes started welling up with tears, I lost it.

I managed to finish reading, but I'm not sure anyone could understand what I was saying through all my blubbering. My sweet husband smiled as he looked at my daughter and me and told me I at least know I made two people cry.

I got some beautiful emails after that story from readers who also had lost their pets and knew all too well the sentiments I was expressing. Then I got an email from the woman I had hoped my message would reach:

"Thank you, Nicole, for posting Amanda Thornton's request to say thank you to a stranger.

"On June 1, I was waiting with my dog in one of the patient rooms at the FM Animal Hospital when I heard a couple come in with their pet. I could hear bits of conversations, and the tone of their voices with the emotional breaks of silence led me quickly to understand what was happening.

"I stayed quiet and held my dog more tightly. I thought of my previous pets and the emotions in their losses. A voice inside me was saying 'somebody should do something to help them,' and then I felt a tug in my heart... it whispered 'I am somebody' and 'I can help.'

"I waited for the assistant to come back to the room I was in and explained what I wanted to do. Her response was a gift in itself. My hand was shaking when I wrote the check, and I asked that the cash be returned to the family.

"It didn't matter if the family would ever know about me, or if they had money or not. I knew at that moment in time that I could try and make a difference in their lives, and maybe, one day, they would reach out to another person to help.

"I have shared that day with my family and friends and explained it as a life-changing moment. Please let Amanda and her family know that I read your article and her thank you. I was moved to help and blessed to have been there at the same time." – Cheryl

A long time ago I wrote a story called "Gold Bikini Girl." This reminds me so much of that story.

While on the surface, I was the one doing the act of kindness by giving a young woman some money, I am truly the one who received from that encounter. You are right, Cheryl, when you follow that little voice inside your heart, an act of kindness can be a life changing experience.

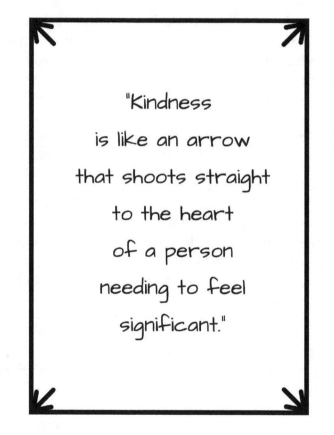

"Kindness
is like an arrow
that shoots straight
to the heart
of a person
needing to feel
significant."

Take Time to T.H.I.N.K.

Do you want to know what terrifies me? The thought of 350 children in a gym with me in charge.

That is exactly the scenario I was faced with a few weeks ago at Longfellow Elementary in Fargo.

The principal called and asked if I would be willing to speak at an all-school assembly on the importance of kindness. I was so excited and flattered when he asked that I honestly started screaming on the phone. "Oh my goodness! Oh my goodness. Really? I would love to!"

That poor man probably still can't hear out of his right ear.

My two oldest kids go to Longfellow, and I cherished the idea of being able to share with them what I actually do for a living while they're gone Monday through Friday. I thought of it kind of like "Bring Your Kid to Work Day," only they wouldn't have to miss any school.

The whole idea of speaking to the students was surrounded by rainbows and butterflies until I realized that I actually had to come up with a message that 1) would be meaningful and 2) would hold the attention of 350 kids ages 5 to 12.

The panic set in.

Thanks to the effort of my entire family, a little help from the Internet, some duct tape and a bag of balloons, I eventually came up with a presentation that was both fun and appropriate for kids.

The day went off without a hitch. The students were incredibly quiet and attentive. No one threw anything at me, and only one child asked if the principal was my boyfriend. I call that a success.

My message for the day was "T.H.I.N.K. Before You Speak." As I was talking with the kids, I couldn't get over the thought that we as adults probably need to be reminded of the same thing.

Many people tell me they are too busy, don't have the money or aren't creative enough to follow through on a daily act of kindness. The truth is, we have the opportunity to be kind every time we open our mouths, and we do that thousands of times a day. We just need to T.H.I.N.K. before we speak.

I'm sure you always think before you speak, so just go ahead and pass this column on to someone you know who could use a friendly reminder.

I found a beautiful acronym on the Internet using the letters T.H.I.N.K.

The T stands for "thoughtful." Before you say something, ask yourself, "Is what I'm going to say thoughtful?" Many times we go about the day thinking of our own needs. We do what is expected of us, but are too self-consumed to even notice that our answers are short and brittle instead of loving and compassionate.

The H stands for "helpful." Again, ask yourself, "Is what I'm going to say helpful?" When you see someone who looks lost or confused, take the extra moment to ask if there is anything you can do to help.

The I stands for "inspiring." Use your words to tell someone about a hidden talent you see in them or a job well done.

The N stands for "necessary." When someone around you messes up, and you respond with "How could you do that?" or "What were you thinking?" you are adding to that person's already low attitude. We usually know when we mess up; we don't need someone to remind us. What we need is someone to say, "It's OK. I've been there."

The K stands for kind. This one is of course my favorite. Taking just an extra moment to make sure you are finding the kindest way to say something can make a huge difference in another person's day.

So, there you have my elementary lesson that I believe pertains to adults as well.

Someone once said, "Everything I need to know I learned in kindergarten." I agree. Sometimes we just need to refresh our memories and T.H.I.N.K.

Shine Bright in a Stranger's Darkest Hour

A few weeks ago I got a last-minute invitation to attend an annual event called "Pray for Gray."

Julie Fletcher began the foundation and the fundraiser as a way to provide hope and support for brain tumor patients and their families.

The project is dear to Julie's heart. Doctors found a pear-sized tumor on Julie's right frontal lobe after she suffered a seizure. Julie was told she could have 12 to 15 months to live. That was six years ago.

Some of the people honored at the Pray for Gray event won't be as lucky as Julie. And they know it. The courage these people show in the face of a devastating diagnosis is enough to bring me to tears.

I went home wrestling with some big questions. I understand I will never know why bad things happen to good people. I have made peace with that. What I want to know is what I can do that will make any sort of difference to someone going through such a difficult time.

Then I got a message from a woman named Bonnie who reminded me that even if we can't fix a situation, we can smooth some of the rough spots.

"Nicole,

Ten years ago, our 17-year-old daughter was diagnosed with a tumor in her pituitary gland. We were looking at multiple tests and trips to the Mayo Clinic, and eventually brain surgery, and then our washing machine broke down.

"Facing one more bill in the midst of the emotional turmoil of our daughter's diagnosis was more than I could bear. I made the comment out loud that I didn't care if I washed clothes on a rock but I wasn't going to charge one more thing on our credit card.

"When we received a bill from the company that came out to deliver our washing machine's death sentence, I decided to temporarily ignore the envelope until I could pay them.

"Sometime later, I got a call from this business spelling out to me that what I received was actually a credit. The woman on the phone explained that I was to come pick out a new washing machine fully paid for by an anonymous donor. The instructions were also to let me know not to get the cheapest one I could, but to get a 'good' one with features that I wanted.

"I wept right on the phone when that angel delivered the news, while wondering who would do such a thing. The nice lady on the phone would not tell me who did it.

"It's 10 years later, and our daughter is a trauma nurse in Texas. Today is her wedding day, and she is back home to walk down the aisle.

"My prayer for Nathan and Nicole is to wish blessings on them that God would continue to care for their every need, even in hard times and that God would abundantly bless that dear person who met our need in a very difficult time."

Thank you, Bonnie, for reminding me that we are here to be the light in times of darkness.

And thank you, Julie, for working so hard to help other brain tumor patients. You have turned your darkest hour into a mission that shines so brightly with your love.

Kindness is a Common Thread in Fight Against Cancer

Five years ago, I went through one of the scariest experiences of my life. I found a lump in one of my breasts.

I made an appointment to see my doctor, truly thinking she'd squelch my fears with the words, "It's nothing."

Instead, she said, "We better get that checked out," and scheduled me for an ultrasound.

The results of the ultrasound pointed to the need for a biopsy. This was it. The outcome of that test could change the course of my life and the lives of my husband and children.

The night before the biopsy, I cried quietly in my husband's arms, thinking for the first time how badly I wanted to see my children grow up.

I shouldn't have gone there in my mind. I should have waited for the test results before I started jumping to my own conclusions. I could have saved myself and my poor husband a lot of heartache because the test came back negative. Life would proceed as before except we would both walk forward with a new sense of gratitude.

My friend Cynthia Eggl went through those same exams. Unfortunately, her tests came back with different results. Cynthia has used her experience to prove that beauty and strength are internal qualities. She is reaching out to other women in her new book, "Boundless Blessings and God's Grace - My Journey through Breast Cancer."

October is National Breast Cancer Awareness Month. I have asked Cynthia to share with you her thoughts on the importance of kindness for those who feel they are walking this path alone.

"When I was diagnosed with Stage 2b breast cancer on April 12, 2011, I placed a framed quote on my dresser in my bedroom. It says, 'You never know how strong you are, until being strong is the only choice you have.' Truer words could not be spoken or read – especially when you are battling for your life, and you are not certain how you will make it one more day.

"During my breast cancer journey, there were several instances that made me realize that God was working through me, even while I was going through this very challenging health ordeal.

"As I sat in the waiting room for my second radiation treatment, the woman sitting across from me and I compared notes, confirming we were both breast cancer survivors who had endured numerous chemotherapy treatments. This was going to be her first radiation treatment, and she was incredibly nervous. I explained in depth what I had experienced the evening before, and thank goodness, I was able to reassure her that it was not as bad as what her mind was envisioning.

"When my name was called, I paused to smile, reach out and squeeze her hand, and tell her not to be frightened. She thanked me, and I felt a calm, peaceful feeling come over me.

"About a week later, my new friend was sitting in a chair in the waiting room when I walked in. She said, 'I'm so glad you are here. I wanted to give you this necklace to thank you for helping calm my fears, making me feel at ease, and leading by example.' She placed the silver necklace, with a silver breast cancer ribbon and a separate pink stone around my neck. I started to cry and gave her a big hug, because she had helped me in the same way. Her gesture was breathtaking.

"For many people, you know that God does work in mysterious ways. About half the way through my radiation treatments in November 2011, I called my car dealership to schedule an oil change.

"When I arrived at the dealership, the gentleman who had walked me through the settings in my vehicle when I purchased it, waved me over to tell me he would give me a ride to work.

"At that time, I was wearing a pink fuzzy cap on my head – my hair was just starting to grow back following chemotherapy treatments. As I stood waiting for my ride, the receptionist looked up and asked if I was a breast cancer patient. I laughed, replied yes, and said my cap must have given it away.

"She asked how my battle had gone so far. She whispered to me that she hadn't said anything to anyone else, but that she was waiting for test results to come back, and she was worried.

"I asked her name, and I said to her, 'I will pray for you.' She asked me my name and said she would pray for me, too.

"The next evening, my driver friend from the dealership called me. He said the receptionist had been diagnosed with breast cancer. She had told him that she was encouraged by my positive attitude and asked him to call me to see if I would talk with her. I told him I would be honored to do so.

"There is little doubt that God was working in my life – through me making the service appointment for my car, the generous offer to drive me to work, which placed me in front of the receptionist's desk for less than five minutes, and then my friend reaching out to me at the receptionist's request. I am happy to report she is doing well, and I have been privileged to be a mentor, so to speak, as she walked the path back to health.

"When we are faced with life-threatening health situations, we realize that within each of us is a fighting spirit and hopefully a recognition that we are not in total control of our lives. We need to accept the difficulties we encounter with dignity, grace, and determination, knowing that God is constantly by our side."

You can purchase Cynthia Eggl's book through her website at www.BoundlessBlessingsAndGodsGrace.com.

Shine Light on the Darkness

I was doing the daily carpool when my 3-year-old son, Ben, piped up from the back seat.

"Mom, what does yannoy mean?"

Yannoy? My brain started turning over every word in Webster's dictionary.

"Yannoy, Ben?"

"No! Annoy, Mom. What does annoy mean?"

As I used words like bother and bug to help him grasp the concept of annoy, I started to think of all the ways I allow myself to become annoyed during the day.

Someone goes first at the four-way stop even though it's my turn. Someone sits at the four-way stop waiting for me to go even though it's not my turn. Someone walks through a door and lets it slam in my face instead of waiting an extra two seconds to hold it open when he can see my hands are full. Someone washes her hands in a public restroom and throws her paper towel on the floor next to the garbage, leaving it for someone else to clean up.

None of these things are tragic, but if I allow myself to start believing that the world is out to steal my happiness, it certainly will.

The Bible talks about going beyond forgiving your enemies and actually wishing a blessing for them. That's always stumped me because I don't feel like I have very many enemies. Who am I supposed to bless if I don't hate anyone?

Maybe my enemy isn't a person. Maybe my enemy is everything in this world that's not light and love. If that's the case, then every day I have the chance to chase away the enemy called darkness, in my life and the lives of the people around me. My weapon is kindness.

Dennis Seeb, a brilliant poet and philosopher in the Fargo-Moorhead area sent me a note explaining how he combats the darkness of people who bump into his happiness.

"A few weeks back I was leaving a local coffee shop. I was already in my car heading out of the parking lot. Here comes another vehicle, and the driver must think I am headed to the drive-thru because instead of slowing down, she actually made a decision to gun it and cut me off so she could get in line ahead of me. Much to her dismay I simply smiled at her as she zoomed by.

"I was not going to let her get away with this kind of behavior. I parked my car and went back into the coffee shop. Thankfully, there was no line inside. I told the barista what had happened and said I wanted to pay for that person's purchase. Then I left. A fleeting moment of grace. It felt pretty good.

"I had a choice at that moment. I chose to continue to have a perfectly nice day. It is just that simple."

Perhaps the woman in the car felt the world was out to get her, that darkness was surrounding her and the only way she could combat it was by kicking into survival mode.

That one act of kindness Dennis paid to a woman who maybe didn't deserve it may have changed the entire outlook of her day and affected the way she treated everyone else she bumped into.

Kindness is contagious. It's also a powerful tool to use against people who yannoy you.

15 Rules for the Game of Life

Sometimes these kindness stories fall into my lap, and sometimes I have to dig a little. The story this week is a combination of both. What I uncovered during my digging took an already great act of kindness (that had fallen into my lap) and turned it into a priceless conversation that left me with way more than I had expected.

Forum reporter Sherri Richards got a story idea from a friend who had seen it on Facebook. Sherri brought it to the attention of my editor, who thought it would be a perfect fit for this kindness column.

That's how the story ended up in my lap, but because not everything you read on Facebook is true, I figured I had better make a few phone calls and do a little more digging.

My first call was to Teresa Lewis, who had originally posted the story online. Teresa explained the turn of events.

Teresa's daughter, Tara, plays basketball for the Liberty Middle School Mustangs in West Fargo. Because of the population explosion in West Fargo, students who have been in class together since elementary school are now finding themselves in opposing colors on opposite sides of the court.

Last year, the girls all suited up together as Cheney Packers. But this fall, with the opening of a new school, the classmates were forced to become competitors.

Now hold on. If you've never been to an eighth grade girls' basketball game, you may be thinking to yourself, "Really? Cut-throat competition at the eighth-grade level? I don't think so." Let me assure you that a win is a win and all who play their hearts out want one, regardless of their age or sex.

Teresa said it was a weird feeling and difficult to figure out when to cheer because she knew so many of the girls on the court.

Even the Liberty coach, Chris Haugen, saw the dilemma. He is a physical education and health teacher at Horace Elementary, so some of the girls on the floor had once been in his classroom.

Coach Haugen decided to use this opportunity to teach his players and former students about true sportsmanship.

Before the game, Coach Haugen gave each of his players a flower. He asked them to walk across the court and hand it to a Cheney player while saying these words, "Teammates last year, competitors today, friends always."

As the game tipped-off, many of the parents and players were still wiping tears from their eyes at this great act of kindness.

When I called Coach Haugen to ask about this series of events, he told me that he feels compelled to equip his students with more than the basics. He wants to help them develop character traits that will last a lifetime.

Then he shared with me 15 principles he has come up with to help kids remember what's important in competition, in the classroom and in life. Now, at awards banquets, he only has to say the first word. The students have taken all 15 rules to heart.

Words To Live By by Chris Haugen, Physical Education Teacher, West Fargo Public School District

1. Play by the rules.

2. Give good effort.

3. Encourage yourself and others.

4. When life knocks you down, get back up and into the game.

5. Success is doing your best; win or lose.

6. Be humble in victory. Don't brag.

7. Be gracious in defeat. Don't whine or make excuses.

8. Be respectful of other people, even though they may not be respectful of you.

9. Share everything that is good, useful or fun.

10. True winners never cheat.

11. If you want to be good at something, practice hard.

12. Say you're sorry when you hurt someone.

13. Look at people's eyes when they speak to you.

14. Put things back where you found them when you're done.

15. Say "Thank you" daily for the many blessings you have received.

I am so thrilled to know we have teachers like Chris Haugen leading the way for our next generation.

Generous Surgeon Heals With Kindness

What did you give people this Christmas? Did you stick to giving those gifts you buy in a store that need to be wrapped and then unwrapped? Or did you go beyond and give them the gift of your love and kindness?

Your talents, your abilities and even your warmth are things they can't get from anyone else.

Pam Nygard from West Fargo shared this extraordinary story of the gift of kindness.

"I hope my story will touch many hearts, especially the heart of the man who made this story possible.

"I am very fortunate to have been so very lucky to have had this experience. I didn't feel so lucky to begin with, but along the journey and in the end, I was the most fortunate person alive to have come to meet someone who opened my eyes to the realization that there truly are good, caring souls out there.

"About two years ago, I went to see a dentist for tooth pain. After X-rays were taken, he discovered an abnormality in another location and referred me to a surgeon specializing in face and jaw surgery.

"I had a cyst in my jaw that had consumed the space where my jawbone had been. The jawbone had actually deteriorated because of the cyst. The surgeon told me that he would need to remove the cysts and then rebuild my jaw with bone from my hip.

"Here's where my story gets interesting. I had no dental or health insurance. To reduce the cost, the surgeon said he could just remove the cyst and see if the jawbone would grow back on its own. That alone would cost at least $4,000. I still couldn't swing it without insurance.

"The surgeon excused himself and his assistant for a few minutes, then returned to tell me his plan. He said, 'This is what we're going to do: We'll take the cyst and see if the jawbone grows back like they did in the olden days.' When I told him I still couldn't afford it, he said he would be doing it with no charge.

"Tears began to roll as I thought of what he had just told me. I was in shock. I felt so guilty and stupid for having a job without benefits. I told him I'd repay him somehow, even if it was little by little, cleaning his office or whatever it took. He said, 'Absolutely not. I want to do this for you.'

"Soon after, he performed the surgery and then the follow-up appointments that required extensive X-rays. It worked. My jawbone had grown back 100 percent.

"What a good, kind man that doctor is. He will never be forgotten. I still shake my head each time I think of him.

"You are truly one in a million, Doc! I hope that someday a truly kind act will, in turn, happen to you."

Kindness, One Dollar at a Time

Is it possible to turn a tragic experience into an opportunity to live more fully and love more openly? Absolutely.

I hear about people who take death, disease and other disasters and somehow find the strength to exhibit kindness through their despair.

I got this letter from a man who went through a very dark time several years ago and ended up learning to be the light.

"I once heard that every curse comes with a blessing but didn't understand it until life-threatening cancer struck without warning. That curse indeed brought unexpected blessings. I wouldn't have chosen to go through the experience, but it's made me a better person.

"The diagnosis came just before Christmas, and I had much less than an even chance of surviving five years. I told my adult children, both of whom had drifted away from the church in which they'd been active as youth, that the only Christmas gift I wanted that year was for them to join my wife and me in worship on Christmas Eve. They did, and it was wonderful.

"On Christmas Day, the four of us carried on our tradition of going to a family movie together. While buying popcorn, I sensed the young lady behind the counter was working on the holiday because her family needed the money. Realizing I didn't know how many more times I'd celebrate Christmas with my family, her sacrifice touched me deeply.

"When she gave me the popcorn, I handed her money equal to twice the order and said, 'Keep the change. Thanks for working today. I hope you have a good Christmas with your family when you get home tonight.' She gave me a startled look, teared up, and said, 'That's the nicest thing anyone ever did for me!' Intuition confirmed, I teared up, too.

"Leaving the theater, I reflected on how an extravagant tip can be such an unexpected kindness. And I didn't have to be wealthy to put the idea into practice. In a restaurant, simply adding $1 above the usual percentage tip would transform it into a resounding expression of appreciation for the service. I resolved to do it as often as my health allows. I rarely see the result, but am confident I've generated many smiles a dollar at a time.

"My new habit unexpectedly led to friendship in another setting. My wife and I subscribe to a concert series and buy discounted parking garage tickets in our package. It dawned on me that this was another opportunity for frugal extravagance as kindness.

"Arriving for the next concert, I handed the garage attendant the usual pre-paid parking stub, but slipped her the amount of the discount, too. She tried to hand it back, but I refused: 'With the discount, I get to park for the regular price and thank you at no extra charge.' She was surprised and grateful.

"At the next concert, I realized that after years of concerts, we knew each other by sight, but not by name. I introduced myself, and she reciprocated. In the following years, we've carried on a conversation, seconds at a time while I go through the garage gate. She asks about my health, and I keep up with how she and her husband are doing. It's become a bonus feature for the concert evening.

"And that's another blessing with the curse: Before the cancer, I rarely went out of my way to establish new relationships. Now I recognize each as a unique gift to myself wrapped in kindness shown to others.

"After aggressive treatment, my prognosis improved dramatically. I'll likely survive well past that five-year threshold that seemed so unlikely at first. But for however many years of good health remain, I'll enjoy surprising people with frugal extravagance and count each opportunity a blessing for myself."

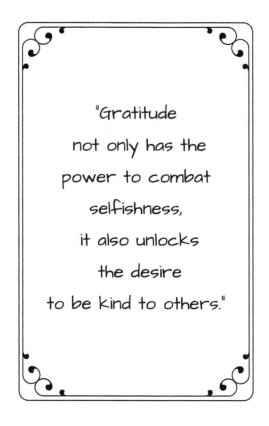

"Gratitude
not only has the
power to combat
selfishness,
it also unlocks
the desire
to be kind to others."

Kindness Through Voicemail

I have a strict personal voicemail system. I keep messages on my phone until I make the decision to a) call the person back or b) ignore the person.

That's the brutal but honest truth. Tell me you don't do the same thing.

But there is one message that has been sitting in my voicemail for more than a year. You see, this message falls into another category: kindness.

Let me set the scene: I had been serving as the volunteer executive director for Diva Connection Foundation (now Women's Impact) for more than a year. I had just worked my tail off writing a grant proposal. The people in charge of giving out the grant money drove to Fargo from Minneapolis to talk with us in person and learn more about the organization. I was psyched. We were incredibly close to taking the nonprofit to a whole new level.

Then the bad news came. We had not been chosen. There would be no money to further our mission, just more blood, sweat and tears as we passionately worked to empower the women in our midst to become leaders in our community.

I was devastated.

That's when I got a call from Pat Traynor. He runs Dakota Medical Foundation and Impact Foundation and was instrumental in getting us off the ground. I heard the phone ring, I knew it was him, and I was too sad to answer.

Here's the message he left on my voicemail:

"Hey, I thought you guys did a great job. I just want you to know, just because a foundation doesn't want to fund you yet doesn't mean that you aren't on to something spectacular and that you haven't done an outstanding job. I just want to tell you that I care. I think you've done an outstanding job, and I think you're a world-class, first-class, top-grade, wonderful and awesome individual. Keep up the great work! I'm proud of you!"

This Fargo man I greatly respect took 33 seconds out of his day to call me, and the words he said meant so much that I haven't been able to let them go.

Your words have power. You have the ability to show great kindness by using those words to lift up the people around you. It costs you nothing and takes less than a minute of your time.

Just in case you are the one who could use some encouraging words today, let me say: You are a world-class, first-class, top-grade, wonderful, awesome individual. Keep up the great work! I'm proud of you!

Maddie's Mission

There is a gas station attached to a coffee shop in north Fargo where I like to write. It's warm, it smells like java and fresh muffins, and there is just enough background noise to keep me on task.

The other day when I walked in, I noticed a man sitting at a table. He didn't have anything to eat or drink in front of him. He was just sitting there. His hair was long, and his face was worn. He had seen the harder side of life.

I thought to myself how kind it was for the managers to let him sit there without buying anything. But then I thought about how uncomfortable I would feel if I were the one sitting there, hearing my stomach rumble and knowing someone was doing me a favor by letting me warm up before it was time to go back into the cold.

I walked over and asked the man if I could buy him a coffee. I'll be honest, it was scary talking to a homeless man. I'm not sure I'd ever done it before, and I wasn't sure the reaction I would get. But when he looked up at me, in his eyes, I saw my maker. I can't explain it really; I can just say that when he accepted the coffee and a little breakfast, too, I had to accept a hard truth about myself: I'm sometimes afraid of the people who need me the most.

I was humbled and inspired to learn about a little girl named Maddie, who at 7 years old, is already serving those who often have the least. Her mom, Kandia, shared this story of how Maddie's Mission came to be:

"This all started for Maddie when we were driving to do errands and she saw a person walking without the appropriate clothing for winter. The wind chill was 20 degrees below zero. The person didn't have a hat, scarf or gloves and was obviously very cold.

"When we got to the store, Maddie saw a box of handwarmers and insisted that we buy them to give out to homeless people we come across in our daily life.

"From that point, everything just sort of snowballed in that little 7-year-old mind, and she ended up coming up with this idea for what she calls 'Stay Warm Packs.' "

"Maddie fills gallon-size zip-top bags with some of the essentials for survival in winter and gives them to homeless individuals. She spent her entire Christmas break making these, taking time to write a message on each one and drawing a cheery picture on the bag for the person receiving them.

"The packs have winter hats, handmade scarves, a box of matches to start campfires, Chapstick, a new pair of socks, a pack of tissues, sports drink mixes, hot chocolate mix (because her little mind rationalized that you can melt snow over your campfire and make hot chocolate), a package of handwarmers, and most recently she has been adding gloves when she can.

"It started out as a simple project that was going to be a one-time thing. Maddie made up 24 little bags and we went to the homeless health clinic to hand them out. While we were there, Maddie got a supportive donation that allowed her to continue her mission.

"When Maddie asked about spreading the awareness of homelessness, we took to social media and started a Facebook page called 'Maddie's Mission.' She posts her activity on there fairly regularly and has me post some awareness things we come across.

"She beams ear to ear when she sees the comments on

Facebook. You can just tell the support helps boost her feeling that what she is doing is indeed good and the right thing to do.

"With the support of people on her Facebook page and in the community, she has continued her project and has made it her mission to help as many homeless individuals as she can to survive and stay warm this winter.

"In total, she has made and distributed almost 100 'Stay Warm Packs.' She has also started collecting hooded sweatshirts and winter coats to take to the Gladys Ray Shelter. She always tells me, I may be little but that doesn't mean I can't help."

Thank you, Maddie, for being big enough to show the people around you what it means to truly love your neighbor.

Join Maddie in helping the homeless at www.facebook.com/maddiesmission2013.

Is Kindness Your First Reaction?

A few years ago, my friend John was driving his brand new minivan when someone barreled into him.

John's first reaction was anger, but before he even let go of the steering wheel, something else took over: compassion.

Somehow, John knew the man in the truck who had just hit him was hurting. Emotionally hurting.

Instead of getting out of that shiny, now-dented, minivan, stomping over to the other driver and screaming, "What were you thinking?" John simply got out of his truck, walked over to the man and said, "Are you OK? What's going on with you?"

The man replied, "I'm so sorry. I shouldn't even be driving. I buried my wife yesterday."

John took the man aside. "This accident is nothing compared to what you are going through. Can I pray for you?"

The two men had a long, meaningful conversation, and both left with more peace than before the accident.

Now, when John gets into his minivan, he remembers the day when anger and accusations were erased by kindness and understanding.

Tracie Overmoe of Moorhead sent me the following letter, explaining how kindness showed up at the scene of her accident, too.

"Nicole, I was waiting to merge into traffic and was suddenly rear-ended. The driver of the other vehicle immediately apologized and admitted it was his fault. I was not hurt but very sore and shook up.

"The driver gave my husband his card and told him to get me a rental car and charge it to him instead of waiting for the insurance. I thought that was odd and wondered if he would really cover the cost. He did.

"God has a funny way of providing for us at times. We had been having some engine problems with our old car, and things were very tight financially. We were limping by hoping our vehicle would hold out until we could get a new one. Since the car was totaled in the accident, we were able to use the insurance money to get a different one.

"A few weeks after the accident, I got a letter in the mail from the other driver. It was a very kind letter of apology and included a generous gift card to a very nice restaurant in downtown Fargo and two movie tickets with popcorn. I had opened the letter in my driveway that morning and was in tears as I read his words and saw his generous gift.

"This was so unexpected and so out of character for how most people would act in a similar situation. I still get choked up when I think about this man's selfless generosity.

"I hope someday I can pay this forward to someone, not in a car accident, but just by doing something so unexpected, so kind, that comes at a perfect time in someone's life to provide the same kind of humble joy we have experienced."

Thank you, John and Tracie, for allowing me to share your stories. Every once in a while, we need to make a snap decision. Will we give in to the emotions that so desperately want to come spewing from our bodies, or will we stop, take a breath and choose to walk in kindness?

Community of Kindness Eases Goodbye

My family is about to go through a period of major upheaval.

My husband, as many of you know, is a basketball coach and most recently got to run all over the court in pure unbridled joy after the North Dakota State University's men's basketball team beat Oklahoma in the NCAA tournament.

Things quieted down for a while – until I got a call last Friday afternoon from my husband saying he would be going to an interview that evening. Just before bed the next night, Saul and I decided it was time to give something new a try.

That was one week ago.

The next day I put our house on the market and then hopped on a plane to spend five days on the campus of Ohio University trying to figure out if Bobcats bite. It turns out, people in Athens are pretty nice, too.

During my 13 years as a coach's wife, I've seen what happens when people break allegiances and head for new schools. People at the old school get mad. And mean.

So when this all went down, I became incredibly scared to answer my phone, open my email or venture into the world of Facebook. I wasn't sure my heart could handle people telling me they thought we were making selfish, money-hungry decisions.

What happened last Sunday morning when the news broke still brings tears to my eyes.

I got a text message from the president of NDSU asking me what he could do to help me make the move less stressful. The president of the school! Where does that happen? Fargo.

I had a girlfriend ask how she could help. When I jokingly said, "Sell my house for me," she did. In five hours. Where does that happen? Fargo.

Another friend came over and literally took clothes out of my closet and put them in my suitcase because I was too overwhelmed to pack for the weeklong trip. Where does that happen? Fargo.

I had more people than I can count taking the time to say they would be praying for my family's smooth transition. Where does that happen? Fargo.

You guys, this community is amazing. Amazing. There is nothing Saul or I have ever done to deserve the kindness shown to us over the past week or over the past 10 years.

You have reached out and touched my heart in such a profound way that I don't even have words to express my gratitude. I just had to use the space in this kindness column to say, "Thank you." You will never know just how much your kindness has meant to me.

Learn Kindness from Jesus

This is the hardest week of the year to write my column. An entire Holy Week culminates with the celebration of Easter.

It should be a piece of cake: Say something about the gift of salvation or tell a sweet story about how someone delivered chocolate bunnies to sick kids, right?

I either go Christian or non-Christian. Make a choice and start writing. While I need to stay true to my own values, I think it's also important to recognize the broad spectrum of beliefs and meet people where they are.

So this year instead of secular or non-secular, I want to try a third option. Let's call it "philosophical."

It is my understanding that most historians agree that Jesus existed and that he may have been the originator of large-scale random acts of kindness.

Jesus was compassionate. He was focused but always took time out of teaching to both heal and feed the people around him. He was honest. He stood up for what he believed and yet was completely submissive to his own Heavenly Father. He also appeared to be quite patient as his popularity grew and crowds of people pressed in on him relentlessly.

When asked what is the most important thing for people to do to live a good life, he simply said, "Love God and love each other."

If you are in a place on your faith walk where you're not able to commit to the "love God" part, then let me encourage you to start with the "love each other" part.

Make a decision before you even put your feet on the ground in the morning to love others. Put Post-It notes on your bathroom mirror to greet others with joy. Be patient with people when they annoy you. Remind yourself that others are hurting just like you, and we could all use a little more gentleness in our lives.

When someone cuts you down, be grateful for the opportunity to work on your humility. Be faithful to your partner and to your promises. Acknowledge that while you have no control over how people treat you, you do have total control over your actions, the decisions you make and the way you treat others, so make self-control a priority.

If we use Easter as a reminder, regardless of our beliefs, to be good, kind, loving people, then Jesus' mission will be accomplished and this world will be a whole lot nicer place to be for everyone.

Whether tomorrow is about a Savior, chocolate bunnies or just another morning to get out of bed, I hope you'll use the day to remember the kindness one man lived long before taking his last breath on the cross.

Creative Kindness to Celebrate Birthday

My birthday is coming up this week. On Wednesday, I'll be 26. Again.

Birthdays are fun, but they don't hold the same excitement for me that they did when I was a child. I remember wanting to invite as many kids as possible over to my house on my birthday in hopes of having a huge stash of presents to open.

Now, I'm a practical and occasionally guilt-ridden mom, so when I receive a gift, I immediately feel badly for all of the work the gift-giver had to go through to bring me said gift. Besides, at a certain point in life, the only things you truly want are a hand to hold and healthy children.

I often hear about thoughtful and creative ways people choose to celebrate their birthdays or the birthdays of loved ones. I got a letter recently from Phyllis, a proud mother, who told me how her son celebrated turning the Big 4-0.

"Dear Nicole,

"Our son, Paul, decided to do something special when he turned 40. He selected 40 people who have made a significant impact on his life and wrote them a letter. These are people who he feels lucky and blessed to have known: friends, family members, colleagues and mentors.

"Enclosed in each of the 40 letters was $11. Eleven is his favorite number, along with the number 4, which are the uniform numbers of his favorite baseball players growing up, Chuck Knoblauch and Lenny Dykstra.

"Here is part of what he said:

" 'First of all, I really do just want to say thanks! My life has been shaped, blessed, and full of some good belly laughs and memories because of these relationships. With the enclosed $11, please make an impact with it.

"Have a coffee date with a spouse or a friend you haven't truly connected with in a while; donate it to someone who needs it; buy flowers for someone; go to a baseball game. I don't care what you do with it, just make a good story out of it!

"Finally, I'm asking that over the course of the next 90 to 120 days, you do something creative with it and report back to me via phone, text or in person.'

"Nicole, I was surprised by his letter and felt it was one of those stories of kindness that you'd like to hear about."

Thanks Phyllis for sharing Paul's story. I'm sure Paul will get to spend the better part of the year hearing about all of the ways his friends thought of to spread the love with $11, and that's a great gift in itself! I'll have to remember that idea when I turn 40. In another 20 years.

Sometimes Kindness Backfires, Sometimes it Changes Your Life

A friend recently asked if kindness ever comes back to bite me. She was struggling with the decision to continue extending kindness to people who just weren't playing along. She felt as if all of her efforts were being done in vain and wondered if it was worth it.

My answer was, "Yes, I've been bitten."

There are times when people are not interested in receiving the love I'm trying to give, but that's OK. I'm not worried about how people treat me or even perceive my actions. I'm concerned with how I'm choosing to treat people.

Sometimes kindness backfires. But as a family in Moorhead discovered, when it hits its mark, it is so worth the risk.

"Hi Nicole,

"I love reading your column and appreciate the hope it brings to our community. In that light, I want to share a 'Kindness is Contagious' moment that recently happened to our family.

"One April day after school, I biked with my young kids to the end of our road to clean up litter. We spent about 45 minutes picking up trash in the green space near the road. It was hard, muddy work, but the kids were huge helpers. We left bags of recycling and trash near the curb (with plans to pick it up later by car) and started biking home.

"Suddenly, I heard a man call out behind me. I slowed down, and a young man on a bike who was probably in his 20s caught up to me. He asked if we had just picked up the garbage from the ground. I said 'Yes,' and he asked to speak to the kids. They turned around on their bikes to visit with him.

"Before I knew what was happening, this young man handed me a $50 bill. He thanked my kids for doing such good work and told them to split the money. I tried to turn it down, but he insisted and biked off with a huge smile.

"We stood there for several minutes so surprised and touched. My kids asked why he gave them the money. I told them that sometimes doing a kind act can make someone else so happy that they want to help out, too. Kindness IS contagious.

"We still don't know who that young man was. If you are reading this story, please know how much your kind gesture was appreciated. You brought huge smiles to the faces of two little kids. Thank you."

My guess is the interaction lasted no longer than two minutes, but those kids will remember that act of kindness for the rest of their lives. Sometimes when you stop to talk to a stranger, it ends up feeling awkward and uncomfortable, but sometimes it ends up creating a lasting lesson in love.

Kindness Found in Reminiscing

I remember two things from the end of my grandfather's life. I was a very little girl, but I remember his eyes and I remember his stories.

His eyes were normally blue, but on this final visit, they were almost turquoise. They were extraordinarily bright, shining, a little damp-looking, and not exactly focused on the people or things in his nursing home room.

I didn't see my grandfather very often as a child, but when I did, I could always count on him for a tall-tale. He loved to tell me about how he almost caught the Easter Bunny and about the year he snuck up on Santa.

The stories he told on my final visit were different. They were true. While my father stood silently next to me, my grandfather told me about how he had just gone on a trip to Chicago, and while he was there, he took in a wrestling match and a visit to a pool hall. He told me I was just as pretty as those lovely ladies who worked in the hall. He was vividly describing something that had happened 50 years earlier as though it were only last weekend.

My grandfather's mind had begun working backwards. Little did I know that for months and months, he had been slowly slipping back into another time period. I just thought he was being funny by telling silly stories. I look back now and cannot even begin to imagine how hard it was for my father to watch his father's mind deteriorate.

Judy Petermann wrote me about her sister-in-law's experience with kindness that reminded me of my grandfather. I'm sure many of you with aging parents or spouses will relate to Judy's gratitude toward a stranger.

"Nicole,

"Recently, Gena, my sister-in-law who thoroughly enjoys visiting, struck up a conversation with a woman seated at a nearby table. The woman was driving alone through Fargo from Williston, N.D., on her way to the east coast to spend time with family. These two women visited about times past, especially focusing on farming memories.

"Both spent their childhoods working on family farms in Western North Dakota and reminisced about the responsibility of bringing cows in from the pasture and milking, as well as cooking tasks at a young age.

"When it was time to part, they hugged and wished each other well. When Gena proceeded to pay her bill, the waiter informed her that the woman she was visiting with had already covered the charge of the meal for both Gena and her husband.

"That woman's kindness extended much further than a free meal.

"Gena's Alzheimer's was diagnosed about 10-15 years ago and was oncoming much before that. Now, when visiting about present day happenings, she needs to ask the same question about what's happening, who will be there, or where we're going every 2 minutes or so.

"The response she seeks only stays with her for a short time, so she needs to ask the same questions again and again. But when visiting about the past, she can continue to stay with the topic and contribute more. Then she enjoys visiting and will even tell remembered jokes.

"The present, however, is difficult. When family or friends are gathered and visiting about issues related to careers, lives, which various family members belong together or even who the newest family babies are, she is lost. She cannot retain that information.

"This can easily bring about depression, because she does have some knowledge of how much she is losing out in family members' conversations including immediate family. Her only means of connecting is when referring to childhood or past experiences. Hence, visiting with a stranger who will engage her is so refreshing for her. Knowing who they are isn't what's important to her.

"This story of sharing preserved memories met the needs of two women who needed companionship: one because she was traveling without family or friends, and the other who got to live in the present while talking about the past."

– Judy Petermann

The real gift given that day wasn't the cost of a meal. It was the precious time spent talking with a stranger who felt like she had found a special friend instead of remembering all that she had lost.

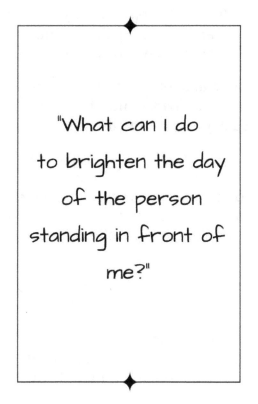

"What can I do
to brighten the day
of the person
standing in front of
me?"

Don't Speed by Your Chance to be Kind

My husband got pulled over for speeding the other day. Mr. Leadfoot has been teasing me for years about what a bad driver I am, so as you can imagine, I was delighted to be in the car witnessing the whole thing.

I'm also pleased to have the opportunity to write about this event in the paper and perhaps publicly embarrass him, so you see I'm not a very kind person after all.

It was just before 8 a.m. on a Monday morning. With three kids and lots of snacks loaded into the minivan, we were ready to begin a day of great thrills.

A man in Fargo (a police officer, actually), told me about Kings Island Amusement Park when he found out I was moving to Ohio. It's near Cincinnati, and he remembered going there a lot as a kid. Since I have a kid who is a roller coaster fanatic, we thought we'd check it out.

Kings Island is about two and a half hours from Athens. We headed out on the back roads, hoping to make good time and get to the park just as it was opening.

Now, back roads in Ohio are not like back roads in North Dakota. They are narrow, twisting, tree-lined, animal-infested and anything but flat. My husband was zooming along without a care in the world as I was stomping the invisible brake and silently praying Bambi and his friends wouldn't choose this moment to leap onto the pavement.

While watching for potential roadkill, I barely noticed the Ohio State Patrol car pass us from the other direction. All of a sudden, though, we were going a lot slower. My husband, like any good driver who sees a squad car, instantly decelerated. Unfortunately, it was too late. The patrol car turned right around, and before we knew it, we were seeing flashing lights.

I started to giggle. My poor husband. It's no wonder he chose a job where he has to be out of town a lot. When he's home he has to deal with me!

When the trooper walked up to the car, it took everything I had not to yell, "Thank you! My husband is constantly calling me 'Gordon Leadfoot'! It's about time he got busted!" But no. I sat silently with a huge smirk on my face.

The trooper walked up to the window looking totally cool in his aviator sunglasses. He asked for Saul's license and then asked where we were going in such a hurry so early in the morning. Saul sheepishly told him we were trying to get to an amusement park.

The trooper took off his shades and peeked at the three wide-eyed children in the back of the van.

"Kings Island? That place is awesome! Have you ever been there before? You guys are gonna love it! Don't forget to ride Banshee – it's new and I've heard it's amazing."

What?! Aren't we supposed to be in trouble right now for breaking the law? Aren't officers supposed to be so harsh and intimidating that they scare you into never breaking the law again?

Saul did get a ticket. He deserved it, and we all knew it. While the officer handed it over, I asked if I could take his picture with my husband. He said he couldn't because he was pretty sure he would get into trouble with his boss if it showed up on Facebook.

And then he smiled.

That state trooper reminded us of two very important lessons: 1) Obey the speed limit, and 2) Your title doesn't have to define how you treat people.

There is always room in every profession to lead with kindness.

Just before we drove off (at a very conservative speed), my 4-year-old timidly piped up from the backseat to ask which one of us had to go to jail.

Nobody today, Sweetheart.

Serving Others Makes 'A Wonderful Life'

Do you remember that movie, "It's a Wonderful Life?" My husband and I watch it every Christmas snuggled up on the couch. I start getting misty-eyed right about the time Clarence, the guardian angel, jumps into the river, forcing George Bailey to save him. When the town comes through for George at the end, I'm an absolute mess. Oh, I love kindness!

That particular movie always reminds me of the words from Hebrews 13:2 (NLT), "Don't forget to show hospitality to strangers, for some who have done this have entertained angels without realizing it!"

Jordan Ohlson is a person who entertains angels. He is a Guest Services Manager at Sanford Health, and recently, he picked up an 81-year-old man who needed a lift. But that was only the beginning of the story.

Jordan shared his experience in a memo to his employees, one of whom was so touched by her boss's act of kindness that she shared it with me.

"Guest Services Team:

"I went to Sioux Falls yesterday. On my way back to Fargo, I noticed an older man walking along the interstate, carrying what looked like a heavy backpack. I pulled over and offered him a ride, which he gladly accepted.

"His name was Clarence, and he had been walking for hours. He explained that he had a spell of bad luck and was trying to get to Fargo, but that he eventually needed to get to Reno, Nevada.

"Long story short, I decided he was a really nice, harmless guy, so I brought him to Fargo and took him to my house. My wife was obviously surprised, but she and the rest of us worked to feed him and do his laundry.

"My kids showed him all their tricks (my kids loved him and he thought they were great), and we let him sleep in our basement overnight. I cooked him breakfast the next day and took him to the bus station where I bought him a ticket and gave him a little cash. Off he went!

"The reason I'm sharing this is because serving Clarence brought a tremendous amount of happiness and satisfaction into my life. It would have been easy not to pick him up. It would have been easy to take him to Fargo, only to drop him off alongside the interstate where he could have continued his journey. I think that's what he expected to happen.

"But I'll tell you what. The joy that my family and Clarence felt would not have been as great if I would have decided to leave him alongside the road upon arriving in Fargo. It would not have been as great if we had decided to only feed him and not provide him shelter. It certainly wouldn't have been as great if we hadn't ensured he had a way to safely travel to his final destination. In doing all this, our intent was to help him, but we may have gotten more out of the experience than he did.

"I know I'm not alone in my philosophy on how we should treat one another. I want to thank all of you for taking the same approach to serving others. Doing so will truly fill our hospitals and clinics with the spirit of service, which will make the Sanford experience one people appreciate. Remember, the joy we and others feel will be proportionate to the time and resources we dedicate to helping others."

Thank you, Jordan, for reminding us that when we live with the goal of serving others through kindness, it truly is a wonderful life.

Boy Turns Mean Joke into Act of Kindness

A Minnesota boy may change the way the medical world uses marijuana.

Brett Solum is a 13-year-old boy who, in many ways, is like a lot of other teenagers. He goes to Moorhead (MN) Middle School where he'll soon be starting seventh grade. He likes the Green Bay Packers, hangs out with the neighbor kids, and has a 6-year-old sister who thinks he hangs the moon.

But there is a difference between Brett and the other kids at school. Somewhere between 45 and 100 times a day, Brett has seizures.

They started out as absence seizures, a short period of time when he would just blank out and stare off into space. Lately, he's been having grand mal seizures, lasting between 15 and 20 minutes each.

Brett's father, Paul, tells me that all of his son's medical options have been exhausted. Brett will never drive a car or even live on his own unless someone discovers a new way to control his epilepsy.

The Mayo Clinic may have a Plan B. Doctors will soon give Brett marijuana drops as part of a study on the drug's effects on young epilepsy patients.

So now that you've got some background information, let me tell you a little more about Brett and what he goes through every day.

Brett arrives at a special entrance to his school where he can enter without the noise and chaos found at the other doors. He immediately turns left and heads directly into his classroom where he spends most of the day with other kids with disabilities.

He has an incredibly kind heart, and while he is totally communicative, his mind does not comprehend sarcasm or teasing. So when a student from another part of the school invited Brett to a birthday party at Chuck E. Cheese, Brett gladly accepted.

His dad took him to Target to buy a gift and then headed to the restaurant. They waited 15 minutes before asking an employee about the reservation, only to find out that there was never a party planned at all. It was a joke. A mean joke by someone who was picking on Brett.

Two weeks later, it was Brett's birthday. His parents told him to invite some friends to go bowling, but it wasn't until they got a phone call from a stranger that they realized how their boy had turned that hurtful fake-party experience into an act of kindness for others.

Brett's parents got a call from a mom asking if they would pick up her daughter on the way to the bowling alley. They picked up the girl at Churches United for the Homeless.

Brett invited kids with severe disabilities, kids who were homeless and kids who just plain felt rejected. He invited kids that no one else ever invites to parties.

We can't control how people treat us, but we can control how we treat others. Brett knows that truth well, and his actions go far in proving that we are not limited by our limitations when we look outside of ourselves and into the hearts of others.

Brett, I don't know much about the medical marijuana controversy, but I do know about kindness. You have shown great kindness to others, and on behalf of everyone who has ever felt left-out, thank you. I'm praying you are touched by a miracle, my friend.

Anonymous Letter Prompts Look for Special People in Our Lives

I remember the first time I saw a $2 bill. I was about 5 or 6 years old, and I thought someone was playing a joke on me.

It looked real, but that 2 in the corner, where the 1 or the 5 or the 10 should have been just seemed so odd. I've run into a few other $2 bills in my life, but not many. It's always kind of a treat, like finding a four-leaf clover or a lucky penny.

The $2 bill was first considered legal tender in 1862, and although the design has changed and printing has stopped and started at various times, it is still a denomination of U.S. currency. Translation? You can still spend it.

I've mentioned before that I have the best writing gig in the world because of the amazing letters I get in the mail. I got one the other day that tops the list and was just "two" sweet:

"Nicole, thanks for sharing your gifts and talents so willingly with others. You are a God-based inspiration to many. Trusting God with all the real scenarios in life and allowing kindness to shine, I'm certain makes God smile and encourages others.

"Enclosed are a week's worth of $2 bills. Give them to whomever God lays on your heart and tell them they are 'too' special!

'This is my small 'pay it forward' plan in thankfulness for the grace bestowed on me by such a loving Savior and for giving me a godly wife for 43-plus years and running. I'm married to my best friend.

"The $2 isn't a monetary windfall, but the words are what Jesus would say to each of us, no matter our situation."

Sure enough, tucked inside that anonymous envelope were seven crisp $2 bills. I had been reading my mail on the living room couch, and I just sort of gasped. I read the letter to my husband and kids and then pulled out the bills. Each child wanted to take a turn looking at them, feeling them, holding them. It was a really neat moment.

Now I have the unique opportunity to create seven more moments. There are so many people who cross my path each day and fill it with light through their kindness that I'm actually having a problem giving the bills away! I haven't been able to decide if I should give them to people who have helped with our transition to Ohio or if I should send them back to people who have touched my heart in North Dakota.

It's hard to know who the perfect recipients should be when I truly feel surrounded by kindness.

And that's the neatest thing about this whole situation: The man who sent me those $2 bills gave me the greatest gift of all. By having to choose seven people who are "too special," he has allowed me to see the multitude of people who show me love, compassion and kindness every single day.

I'm certain the people to whom I end up giving the bills will think it was a sweet gesture, but they will never know that by being the conduit, I actually became the biggest recipient. I was forced to slow down and contemplate just how many people go out of their way to make my life better.

If you can manage it, I hope you'll play along with me. Get seven crisp $1 bills (or $2 bills!) and carry them around until your heart tells you to give them away, one at a time. I suspect it will open your eyes to the number of people who shine with goodness in your life.

Kind Gift Helps Couple Celebrate Anniversary

I never wanted to get married. I didn't believe in the institution of marriage. I honestly thought it was impossible for a man and a woman to remain faithful to each other for a lifetime.

I dated. I eventually wanted children. I hadn't worked out all the details, but I was certain marriage would not be part of the equation.

I'm not sure what happened. It's almost as if God stepped in and said, "OK, that's enough of that foolishness. Here's your husband." And as quick as that, I was in love with Saul and was willing to face whatever lay ahead, as long as I could face it with him. It never occurred to me again that we wouldn't be faithful. We were meant to be together, and that was that.

I still count Saul as the greatest blessing in my life. Boy, am I thankful for divine intervention.

In a few days we will be celebrating 14 years of marriage. Like any married couple, we have our moments. It bugs me when he snores. It bugs him when I nag.

In some ways, we are an old married couple, but we both realize we are still newlyweds by many standards, especially when compared to the man who wrote me about his recent anniversary celebration.

"Dear Nicole,

"I am writing to inform you of an act of kindness that recently happened to my wife, Judy, and me.

"Judy was diagnosed with Alzheimer's in 2008. I have taken care of her at home for six years now. The good people of hospice have helped me for the past year. I made Judy a promise when she was diagnosed that I would take care of her as long as I could. So far, the Lord has given me good health, and I will continue to care for her until He calls her home or my health will no longer allow it.

"We celebrated our 50th wedding anniversary on May 16. I set up an appointment with the hair salon that Judy has gone to since we moved to Fargo in 1998.

"I have been able to take her to her weekly hair appointments during this entire time. Her hair stylist, Janelle, the owner of West 13th Salon in West Fargo, thought it was special that I would bring her in on the morning of our anniversary.

"When she got done styling Judy's hair, she got her camera out and asked if she could take a picture of us. About two weeks later, when I brought Judy in for her hair appointment, Janelle handed me a gift and said it was for our anniversary. It was the picture of us that she had taken. It was in a special 50th anniversary frame with the following inscription on it: 'It doesn't matter where you go in life, it's who you have beside you. Happy Anniversary Bill and Judy.'

"It is a wonderful gift. I thought it was so special that Janelle would go to all that time and expense to give us that gift.

"Those are the kinds of things that happen in the Fargo-Moorhead area and West Fargo area. It's a great place to live."– Bill Sunderlin, Fargo

There is great kindness in doing the little things in life well. Like caring for the one you love each and every day. In sickness and in health. Till death do you part.

Happy anniversary to the man who was (and is) the best gift I've ever gotten.

Why Me?

Several months ago, when we left North Dakota for Ohio, we moved into a lovely home tucked into a quiet, wooded neighborhood in the city of Athens.

Just before you turn to go up the hill into our subdivision, you pass a little log cabin. On first glance, it's beautiful. Very shabby-chic. On second glance, it's a whole lot more shabby than chic.

With no other children in the neighborhood, it wasn't long before my kids made fast friends with the kids living in that cottage down the hill. Now, instead of having a clean, quiet, orderly household, I have noise. Lots and lots of noise made by lots and lots of kids. Luckily, the most predominant noise is usually laughter.

I don't know much about life in that little log cabin, but I know there are more people under the roof than there are beds. I know the youth football coach comes to pick up the little boy because the woman everyone calls "Grandma" doesn't have a car. And I know that the kids call themselves "cousins" because it's easier than explaining how they all ended up in the same house when few of them are related.

Sometimes I hear that their phone is turned off, their TV isn't working or Grandma is having a yard sale because there is no money for birthday presents and it makes me sad. Why do I get to live in the lovely house at the top of the hill while they are stuck at the bottom? But standing still and being sad doesn't help anything. So I do what I can.

I have gone from a mom who rarely cooks anything that isn't in a box to a mom who is constantly at the grocery store loading up on fresh fruits, veggies and protein so I can feed my kids and a few others who happen to be in the house for either lunch or dinner on a daily basis.

I have gone through my kids' clothes and shoes and given our abundance to our new friends.

I have donated a closet-full of household decor to the garage sale in hopes of fattening the bottom line and raising more birthday present money.

But in the midst of my personal crusade of kindness, I realized something. My acts of kindness don't even touch the amount of kindness once again being shown to us.

While I was so busy trying to help our new neighbors, I barely noticed how much they were helping us. Those children have surrounded my kids with such nonjudgmental love, fun and laughter. They have introduced my kids to new friends, made them feel like part of the gang and have helped to smooth the transition to a new town.

I wanted to say thank you, so – as uncomfortable as it was – I marched right up to the front door of that little log cabin and asked Grandma if I could buy the children new backpacks and school supplies. I was terrified she would be offended, but I desperately wanted the kids under her care to be able to walk into school with all of the things I knew they wouldn't be able to afford on their own.

When all was said and done, I had seven kids loaded into the car, a trunk full of notebooks, folders, pens and erasers and a very long cash register receipt. I couldn't have been happier or felt more blessed to have been able to share our blessings.

We can't change someone's lot in life, but we can make their life a lot more enjoyable by leading with kindness. When we do, it makes our lives a lot more enjoyable, too.

Kind Words Help Frazzled Mom Remember She's Not Alone

There is a unique solidarity among coaches' wives.

Coaches' wives get the fact that our husbands watch tape until 2 a.m., and that they are on recruiting calls while we are on vacation, and that they walk around a little grumpy the day after a big loss.

Coaches' wives who are also moms understand something else: We often parent alone.

I pride myself on being independent, on being able to get the kids from Point A to Point B every single day and perhaps even teaching them some life lessons along the way.

During the basketball season, I spend so much time in my "I am woman hear me roar" zone of solo parenting that when my husband is home, I get angry with him for throwing off our routine. It usually takes me about a week after tournament time to adjust to co-parenting again. The poor man now knows to just ride it out.

I'm sure there are lots of women who can relate: military wives, single moms, spouses of traveling businessmen. The circumstances may be different, but I think we probably go through many of the same emotions. We are proud of what we can accomplish on our own, but sometimes we are just plain worn out and need some help.

I have one new group to add to my little sorority: pastors' wives. My friend Maria, whose husband is a pastor, shared with me an experience she had in Fargo this summer with her four small children.

Maria's husband may not be watching tape and taking recruiting calls, but I bet he spends a good amount of "free time" planning sermons and making hospital visits.

And I know that while Maria is proud of her independence, she is certainly grateful for helping hands.

"We needed groceries on perhaps the hottest day in July. It was stifling hot, but we were out of almost every snack and basic food in the house, so, after the toddler's nap, we headed to the grocery store.

"That particular hot day reflected my son's mood perfectly. He was grouchy. We got near the watermelon, and he started saying 'apple.' I explained they were watermelon and that we'd have to pay for them.

"Things went downhill from there, so we shopped the produce section with a toddler shouting 'Apple! Apple!' in the most pathetic 'please can't I have an apple' tone that you ever did hear. I stayed fairly calm on the outside but had made the decision to get just a few more items and beat it out of the store.

"When we got over to the grapefruit/orange section, an elderly woman leaned down to my little boy, who was in tears, and told him his shirt was 'sure nice' and asked him where he got it. As his tearful shouts of 'apple' subsided, my tears nearly fell because the woman reminded me of how my grandma might have calmly talked to a little person in a store.

"My son didn't answer the lady, but he smiled and calmed down after she visited with him. I guess he just needed his mind taken off the forbidden 'apple.'

"We ended up getting our entire list thanks to that kind woman who helped out a sad little boy instead of just staring and shaking her head.

"I hear of other people getting that kind of reaction, and I wonder if I just don't notice when it happens to me or if I'm just somehow blessed to find all these really kind people in my path! Either way, I want to be like that elderly woman someday."

They say it takes a village to raise a child, and I'm so thankful when I run into those people who, with just one kind word, remind me I'm not alone and help to hold down the fort until Daddy gets home.

Kindness Paves Road to Miss America

Seventeen years ago this very weekend, I competed in the Miss America pageant representing my home state of Wisconsin.

When the pageant was over, I came home with an interview award, $10,000 in scholarship money and a whole bunch of sparkly earrings (some of which are still in my jewelry box).

When people ask how I did, I like to tell them I won 11th place. In my day, they only announced the top 10 finalists, so I feel I can safely assume I must have been 11th.

The thing about Miss America is that you only get one shot. Once you've been on that stage, you can never compete again. You have to give it all you've got, which is hard when you have no idea what the playing field even looks like in real life.

I had never been to Atlantic City, N.J., until I showed up for the pageant, so I had to rely on my committee and trust they would prepare me for the unknown.

I remember staring blankly at my traveling companion who was on her knees on her living room floor laying out every outfit I would wear for two whole weeks, complete with underwear, jewelry and shoes. Then she started labeling everything "Miss Wis." It wasn't until I was in a dressing room with 49 other contestants that I realized this was not her first rodeo. I'm certain her kindness and great attention to detail is the only reason you couldn't see my undies on national television.

Of course, the Miss America program is about so much more than hair, clothes and nails. It's about giving young women at every level of competition the chance to speak about an issue that has become their personal ministry.

Mine was "Overcoming Crisis." I spent the year talking with kids about what to do when life rolls over you with those big, turbulent messes like divorce, death and moving. I can't promise I changed the world, but I still have letters from several high school kids telling me I changed their lives.

I know I wouldn't have been in that position if it hadn't been for all of the people lifting me up and acting as my personal cheerleaders for that one magical year.

Now it's someone else's turn. Jacky Arness is our current Miss North Dakota. On Sunday night, she will step out on that Miss America stage for the final night of competition. This Fargo girl will give it all she's got, and if she wins, you'll hear me screaming all the way from Ohio. But even if she doesn't, she'll come home and continue to change her part of the world, one life at a time through her platform of empowerment.

I know Jacky is feeling the same support and love I felt 17 years ago, and so is her mom, Amy, who wrote me this letter about the kindness that is surrounding their family:

"Just when Jacky is feeling fatigued, discouraged, like she can never accomplish enough, or be prepared enough, we will receive something from a friend or even a brand-new acquaintance.

"We've gotten messages of encouragement and overwhelming offers of generosity, including a year of massage services, a year-long lease on a car, nutritional supplements, personal training, dietician expertise, a restaurant willing to host a fundraiser, a theater willing to donate space for a send-off party, a private plane ride to Williston to be at an important state-wide event, gas cards for travel and restaurant meals.

"It all helps defray the many costs of preparing a girl to be on a somewhat level playing field with these other 'pageant' states that get huge amounts of support.

"There are moments when I as a mom feel I need to be 10 people in order to provide the assistance needed, and then something will happen that will cause me to pause, get choked up, and sometimes literally have to sit down on the ground right where I am because I am so overwhelmed with gratitude!"

I remember feeling that way, too, Amy. Thank you for sharing.

These days I watch the pageant from the sidelines (aka my living room couch), while eating ice cream, but reading Amy's words and thinking about the emotions her daughter must be feeling right now bring me back to my own year as Miss Wisconsin. It was a special time filled with special people and more kindness than a person could ever imagine.

Kindness Makes World of Difference to Newcomer

Have you ever had a life experience in which you thought to yourself, "If I can just live through this, it'll all be OK?"

I have had several, and I'm a little embarrassed to say they weren't caused by the bad things in my life. They were caused by the good things. Those moments of acute anxiety were caused by things I actually wanted. It's like wanting to be in the pool, but freaking out when the water gets waist-level because it is so excruciatingly cold. You know once you're submerged you'll be fine, but getting there is going to be a battle.

One of my "If I can only live through this..." moments was my first day on the job as a television traffic reporter in Milwaukee. I was 22 years old, and I truly thought I was going to have heart-failure when that TV camera light flashed "ON." Once I made it through that first show, I was hooked, but boy was it a scary start.

Another of my "If I can only live through this..." moments happened my junior year of college when I was studying in the south of France. Actually, it wasn't just one moment. It was an entire year of moments.

I went to France full of fanciful ideas of how I would wear skinny jeans and berets, sip espressos at outdoor cafes and speak fluently with all of my new French friends.

The reality was that I stuck out like a sore thumb in a beret, coffees at cafes were too expensive to drink more than once a month, and I could barely speak enough French to order a croissant.

I was lonely, poor and lost. What I would have given for

someone to take me under their wing and help me feel at home.

I did meet someone at a park once who smiled sweetly and spoke slowly, but then he followed me back to my dorm and I had to call security.

Living through the experiences of that year away has given me new eyes for people who are out of their element. It has taught me to be especially kind to those who are finding their way in our country.

David Buchanan of Fargo sent me this story about a colleague who went out of his way to welcome a newcomer.

"One of our North Dakota ag producers was on a flight into Fargo from Chicago last month and was sitting with a young woman who turned out to be a student from Germany coming to North Dakota State University for the first time.

"The flight was delayed, so she was concerned that the NDSU people who were to meet her would not stay at the airport until the flight arrived. He assured her that he had a car and would be happy to take her to the campus if need be.

"When the flight arrived, he saw that the NDSU people were still there, so he watched to make certain that everything was OK for her, said goodbye and turned to leave. The young woman ran after him to give him a hug and ask for his contact information.

"The next day she called him to ask if he could serve as her emergency contact. This was required for her to complete her registration. He asked for her family contact information so that, in the event that he did need to serve as her emergency contact, he could contact her family.

"She then asked him if she could come out to his farm to visit him and his wife sometime.

"A simple airplane conversation and an offer to deliver her from the airport to NDSU turned into an excellent first impression for a foreign student coming to the United States."

I have no doubt the young woman in this story will still have moments this year in which she will say to herself, "If I can only live through this…" but perhaps because of the kindness of a stranger they will be far fewer than one might expect.

Sometimes Kindness Means Extending the Olive Branch

I am the youngest of 50 cousins. I have several hundred second-cousins, but please don't ask me to name more than 10 of them.

The last family reunion was held at a park in Wisconsin and was a bit of a community event. It's always hard to tell who is really part of the family and who just showed up because they smelled the grill. Throw on a name tag. We'll feed you.

I recently realized my dad has a brother I never knew existed.

My dad, being the second-youngest of 11 children, has seen too many of his siblings pass away. He is in his 70s, and he longs for both connection and reconciliation at this point in his life.

I've written before about the role kindness plays in serendipitous events. Well, three times over the course of just a few weeks in three very unusual places, my dad happened to be talking to people who took notice of his last name.

One was at a bait-and-tackle shop. One was at an eye doctor, and one was while he was just out taking a walk.

All three times, people said, "Locy?" (It's pronounced low-C.) "Locy? Do you know Wayne Locy?"

"That's my brother!" my dad replied. Through those three conversations, my dad learned about his brother's health, children and general well-being.

During the third conversation, my dad found out his brother has a daughter who is an electrician. It just so happened my dad needed an electrician, so he called her up.

The day Wayne's daughter was supposed to show up at my dad's house to do some electrical work, she brought along a surprise.

Her dad.

My dad was shocked but so incredibly grateful to get a chance to sit and visit again with his long-lost brother. He said it was an amazing reunion.

I asked my dad whatever happened between him and Wayne, why they had a falling out in the first place. His answer was heart-breaking. He said, "I don't know. They stopped showing up to things we invited them to, so we stopped inviting them."

That was it.

No major argument or disturbance. Just two people on two different sides of the fence who both probably got a little offended once by something someone did and didn't even mean to do and then they just slowly stopped talking. Forever.

Uff da. It knocks the wind right out of me.

Let me ask you this: How easily are you offended? How difficult would it be to pick up the olive branch and extend it, even if it meant you had to apologize for something you didn't even do? What sort of love and light would it let into your life if you took the risk?

Sometimes being kind means turning the other cheek, picking up the phone, and simply calling the right electrician.

You can wait for a string of serendipitous events, or you can create them on your own with kindness.

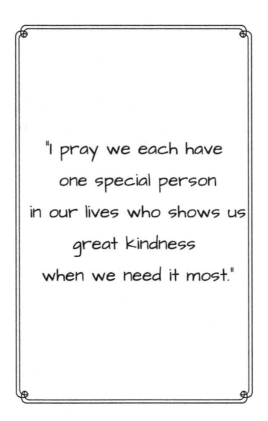

"I pray we each have
one special person
in our lives who shows us
great kindness
when we need it most."

One Special Friend to Show Kindness

Have you ever felt like everyone was in on a joke except you?

I'm not sure if I should feel angry or sad, but deep in my heart, I'm feeling a strange combination of dark emotions that are all jumbled together and desperately striving to find the light.

And it's all the result of a third-grade birthday party.

My son goes to school with a little girl whose momma is in prison. Through a course of odd events that I often seem to find myself in, I've become pretty close with this little girl. She is a bubbly, blond-haired wisp of a child, slight in stature but bold in personality.

When I found out my young friend was turning 9, I did what I do with all little girls whose mommas are in prison. I threw her a pizza party to celebrate her special day.

Birthday girl and I went to Walmart, where we found Monster High plates, cups and party favors. Then we came back to my house and sat at the kitchen table, where we carefully penned 10 Monster High invitations, one for every girl in her class. We filled zebra-print goody bags (24 of them so there would be enough if little brothers and sisters showed up). Her grandma ordered a huge Monster High cake, and we anxiously awaited Birthday Party Day.

The day of the party finally arrived. We ate pizza, played games, blew out birthday candles and opened presents. The hour and a half came and went before I realized something everyone else probably already knew: None of the kids were coming.

I thought it was odd that only one classmate returned an RSVP, but I brushed it off.

I couldn't brush off the fact that only the third-grade teacher and Birthday Girl's one best friend came to the party.

People are busy. I get that. But ALL of them? Every girl in the class, except one? I have a little trouble believing that.

I asked the teacher what I was missing. Clearly there was something going on that I didn't know about.

As my heart started breaking, the teacher gently explained that perhaps the girls never even showed their parents the invite because they didn't want to come to this particular party. She trailed off sadly with, "You know how it is..."

Oh God. Yes. I do know how it is.

I went home, took a warm bath and cried. I cried for so many reasons, but mainly I cried because I saw so much of myself in that outcast little girl.

And then, as my husband sat snuggling me in a fuzzy blanket, I remembered something else the teacher said to me.

She said, "You don't need a lot of friends in this world. Just one."

That's right. That's when kindness truly shines its brightest. When the world seems dark and then you have that one true friend who shows up to your birthday party, and all of sudden, you couldn't care less if anyone else in the world even existed.

I pray that we can all teach our kids to be kind to the outcasts, but until that day comes, I pray that we each have one special person in our lives who shows us great kindness when we need it most.

Overwhelming Kindness Requires No Thank You

I had a friend once whose little boy was diagnosed with cancer. During that dark journey, the family was forced to rely on community support in almost every aspect of their lives. Medical bills, car payments, child care and homework delivery were all handled by a team of people who just wanted to help.

I watched that little boy slowly deteriorate and then gradually regain his life, but what I remember most is one particular conversation with his mom.

She told me she felt guilty over the outpouring of kindness because she worried she could never repay all of those people. She said even the thought of expressing her thanks to that many people was exhausting.

I got a letter from a woman named Marilyn Ouart who can probably relate to my friend's feelings of being overwhelmed by kindness. Life got unexpectedly hard for Marilyn several years ago, but the amount of kindness she has seen since then continues to lift her up and give her family strength.

"In January 2008 my husband, Rusty, was deployed to Iraq. In May of that year, he was injured from an incoming mortar to his fob (barracks). He was thrown, hit with shrapnel and suffered a traumatic brain injury.

"Rusty cleaned himself up and continued suffering with headaches, vomiting, confusion and bloody noses. A month later, he passed out in the Humvee, and when he came to, he was throwing up and had trouble speaking. It was thought he had a stroke and was sent back to the U.S. After months at Fort Lewis, WA, Rusty returned home in January 2009.

"Once home, Rusty traveled to New Orleans for Hyperbaric Oxygen Treatments, spending two months each time.

"This was not covered by his health insurance, but with the help of our community hosting a fundraiser, it was made possible. Rusty continues to have many health issues related to his injury, such as headaches, vertigo, vomiting and trouble with cognitive thinking, but thanks to those treatments, my husband can walk and talk again.

"I continue to be thankful to those who help when possible and to those who remember our soldiers and their families.

"This letter was hard to write because it's difficult to name all of the people and businesses who have shown us kindness: the dentist who gives us discounted services, the pool people who exchanged our pool for a better one, the multitude who came through when lightning struck our home in July 2010 and we lost everything in a house fire.

"There have been so many angels of kindness to our family in this community, but I'd like to tell you about the most recent.

"A few weeks ago, our riding lawn mower had steering problems, so I took it to the dealer in Moorhead. I borrowed a trailer from my brother-in-law who helped me load it, and off I went to RDO to get it fixed. When I got the quote of the price to fix it, I struggled with how to make this work on our budget but ended up giving the OK. I have teenage boys who mow lawns in the summer, so getting it fixed was important to them.

"When I went to pick up the lawn mower, I was greeted by five friendly employees. They had sharpened the blades and fixed some additional problems with the mower. I proceeded to take out my checkbook but was told to put it away as this was a 'no charge.'

"They told me to make sure to thank my husband for his service. It took all I had inside not to show my grateful emotions with tears. Again, we thank the community of Fargo-Moorhead for its unending generosity and kindness."

Marilyn, thank you for sharing your story and allowing others to experience the gift that comes from helping others.

Choose Kindness Even at the Cellphone Store

Do you want to know the problem with making kindness your mission in life? You actually have to be kind. All the time.

The other day, my husband and I were having problems communicating. Since it was more of a technology issue than a marital issue, we headed into the cellphone store to straighten it out. Saul's not big into reading the fine print of contracts (or listening as others are explaining the fine print), so a few months prior, he had agreed to a cell plan we neither wanted nor needed.

We marched into the store a bit out of sorts. We were both upset about the situation but not quite sure on whom our fury should land.

We had planned to demand to speak to the manager, but it turned out we never had to. She greeted us at the door.

I try to swallow my darker emotions and choose kindness, but sometimes it's hard. That said, instead of pointing fingers at this manager or any of her employees, I just tried desperately to explain our conundrum in the hopes she could make it all better.

She did.

As we were finishing the final paperwork, she looked at me and said, "So, what do you do?"

"I'm a writer," I said.

"Oh! What do you write?"

And this is when I was so thankful I had chosen not to enter the store on the attack. "Kindness," I sheepishly answered.

She asked where she could read my column, so I gave her the website. Not only did she read it, she actually sent me a story that reminded me why it's important to treat everyone we meet tenderly. Because when we're done with our "day job," we each still have to deal with the joys and sorrows of real life.

Here's Valerie's letter:

"My grandmother is not doing well. Recently, while in the emergency room, a man came around and was picking up the trash in each room. I smiled at the man and asked him how his day was going. We made small talk about the work day and when he started to leave, I told him to have a good evening. He thanked me.

"About an hour later, I noticed the man passing by the room again. He came back into our room and told me that out of 18 rooms, I was the only person who spoke to him. He said I didn't just talk to him, but I smiled at him and asked him how he was doing. He thanked me again and said, 'God bless.'

"I wanted to jump out of my seat because I saw kindness displayed and just felt good. Have we as a society become so consumed with ourselves that we can't even say hello to a man who is working to change our trash cans? I hope not and promise to continue to display acts of kindness!"

Valerie, thank you so much for sharing your story. That "jump out of my seat" feeling is exactly the reason I started writing this column three years ago.

Thank you, also, for helping this husband-wife team improve our communication!

Friendship and Kindness Can Cure Anything

It's been six months since the moving truck pulled out of my driveway in North Fargo and made the 16-hour trek to Athens, Ohio.

Six months. That seems like such a long time. By all outward appearances, we are settled into our new life: my husband's face is on posters all over town announcing the basketball schedule; my kids have play dates and cross-country practice; I go out for coffee with friends and volunteer at the elementary school; I've even hosted a Bible study in my home.

Every box is unpacked, and the pictures are hung on the walls. My home looks like a home. I thought I had everyone fooled, but leave it to a 10-year-old to call you out on the facade.

The other night when I tucked my daughter, Jordan, into bed, she asked me a curious question. She said, "Mom, are you alright?" I told her that I was fine, just a little tired from the day and that it was time to get some sleep, but as I kissed her forehead, I knew that wasn't what she was asking.

I strive to have the kind of relationship with my children where they are free to say what's on their minds, so I reopened the can of worms the next morning.

"Jordan, about last night... what did you mean?"

She went on to say that she senses a difference in me. She said I don't seem as happy and free and light as I was in Fargo. She said the last time she saw me like that was when my best friend from Fargo came to visit in August.

It was a punch to the gut. Tears started leaking from my eyeballs before I could tell them to stop.

As a mom, I think that if the dishes are clean, the laundry is put away and everyone has a note in their lunchbox when they head out the door, then no one will notice if I'm a little out of sorts.

I was in such a rush to unpack boxes and check things off my to-do list that I forgot how moving takes an emotional toll. Or maybe I thought if I just kept busy I wouldn't have to feel it.

Here's where the kindness comes in. After Jordan left for school that day, I texted my best friend from Fargo and told her what happened. I shared with her things I hadn't shared with her or anyone else in a long, long time.

She reminded me that I'm still an important part of her tribe. She said, "You are the part of my tribe that makes me look differently at the world and the people in the world. I want to be a better person because of you."

She reminded me that I'm still the same person I was even though I go to sleep in a different town and still get lost sometimes on my way to the grocery store. It felt so good to just let down the walls and be honest about what I was feeling.

When was the last time you've done that? Totally surrendered and admitted that you don't have it all together? Our vulnerability is a great gift to others because it creates a safe space for them to be honest, too. That's the space where kindness lives.

Later that afternoon, as I was sitting in my quiet house, the doorbell rang. Flowers. My girlfriend sent me flowers to remind me that friendship and kindness can cure anything – even homesickness.

Handyman's Act of Kindness Changes His Life

A man came to my house the other day to repair all of those little things in a home that are too difficult to fix myself, yet not so difficult that they involve cutting my losses and just moving.

He actually came the first time to convince the mice who had moved into my basement that they'd be better off finding a new place to make their winter nests. While he was here, he mentioned that he used to build houses, but left that life to instead chase away bats and mice as an exterminator. He said he still enjoys puttering around houses and fixing things.

Fixing things? Big mistake mentioning that, Mr. Exterminator.

Before he knew it, I had talked him into coming back 10 days later and pressed a laundry list of to-do things into his hand so he'd be able to return with all the right tools.

Now, let me just stop and say I noticed something special about this man right away. I couldn't put my finger on it, but there was a certain light, a certain joy and peace that seemed to radiate from him.

When he came back to fix the roof, the faucet and recheck the mice, I noticed that light again. And again, I couldn't put my finger on it.

We sat down at the kitchen table to settle up the bill at the end of the day. As I began writing the check, I asked, "What's the date?"

"Nov. 4," he said. "My brother called me this morning to remind me."

Huh? I looked at him quizzically, because none of my family members call me to remind me what day it is (although perhaps they should sometimes).

He went on to tell me that three years ago, on Nov. 4, he gave his brother one of his kidneys. His brother calls him every year on that day to tell him thank you.

I had never met anyone who'd been a donor before, so I went on to ask the usual questions. Did it hurt? Is your brother OK?

He said it didn't hurt and his brother was fine. Then he said something that shed great light on this inner peace I saw radiating from his eyes.

He said his brother was really sick and desperately needed the kidney, but that being the one allowed to make that donation changed his own life, perhaps even more than his brother's.

He said making that decision forced him to evaluate how he was living. He found some things he didn't like and decided to change them. He quit his job and started doing what he loved: chasing little creatures from people's homes. He stays busy enough to put a daughter through college, but he also has time to go pheasant hunting for a week, and do odd jobs just because he feels like it.

He said his life may be shortened by a year or two without a second kidney, but that's OK because he's living each day to the fullest. He said he sees every sunrise and every sunset with new eyes and a new sense of wonder. He appreciates the beauty in this world that he was too busy or too bothered to notice before.

As I listened to him, I couldn't help but think of you, reading this column, and my weekly attempt to convince people that life is better with kindness. This man is a walking testimony for what I'm trying to get through to the world: when you help others, you help yourself. One act of kindness, in this case, one kidney, bought his freedom from the daily grind.

I handed my insightful handyman the check. He smiled and said, "I'm gonna spend this money frivolously. I'm going to buy a ukulele. I've always wanted to learn how to play."

I laughed and said it was the best money I'd ever spent.

Season of Thanksgiving Unlocks Kindness

The other night I put my kids to bed an hour and a half before their regular bedtime so I could sit on the couch, eat Ben & Jerry's and watch a Hallmark Christmas movie alone in silence.

I'm not sure what kind of message that is sending to my family, but I'm sure it's not a good one.

I've got a pretty thick selfish streak. Part of me hopes you do, too, so I know I'm not the only one. The other part of me hopes it's just me. I told you, I'm selfish.

At this point in my life, my selfishness manifests itself mainly in areas dealing with comfort and convenience. I don't want to have to "suffer" through anything, and I don't want to use my time doing something I'd rather not be doing.

For example, I didn't do any Black Friday shopping because I don't like to miss my full eight hours of sleep, and I don't want to be bothered by crowds, bad parking and long check-out lines.

I would rather stay in the comfort of my own home and pay more when I venture out next Tuesday than to be inconvenienced so severely for a few really good deals.

Now that I think about it, though, staying home might not make me selfish. It might just make me smart.

Seriously though, when it comes to dealing with my husband and my children, I am pretty selfish. They all know, "It's momma's way or the highway."

The funny thing is that they allow me to be this way. The kids are still young, so what I say goes – even when it doesn't make much sense. And my husband, Saul, just wants to keep the peace, so he lets his wife pretend to be in charge.

But I know I'm wrong, and I'm working on it.

The war against selfishness starts with a little notebook next to the chair in my office. It's a gratitude journal. I hope someday to have filled every line on every page with things I'm grateful for, but right now I'm only at No. 402, which means I still have three-fourths of the book to go.

Journaling my blessings is much harder than I had anticipated. Once I got past the house, family, health and car, it became incredibly difficult to put into words those things for which I am grateful.

Some of them are flippant, like No. 6: "Dogs that sleep with their feet straight up in the air." I wrote that one down because it makes me laugh when I'm in my office so engrossed in what I'm typing and then glance over to see my two golden-doodles sleeping in some bizarre, totally uncomfortable position.

Some are more serious, like No. 193: "That there is more grace in you, God, than there is sin in me."

And No. 196: "That someone I don't even know would read my words and send money to help my neighbor in her time of need."

When I look back at my journal, I realize that gratitude not only has the power to combat selfishness, it also unlocks the desire to be kind to others. I re-read what I've written, and I want to put others first because I realize how much I've been given. I am renewed from a place I can't even identify.

I hope you have quiet moments today to really reflect on what you're thankful for. You might even want to write them down so you can go back and remind yourself of those special gifts later, when life gets hard.

If you get through the entire day without having a single moment to yourself, feel free to send everyone to bed an hour and a half early. You won't hear me calling you selfish.

Job Seeker Finds Big Kindness on Facebook

Sometimes social media is nasty. I mean really, truly, ruin-a-person's-day nasty. It gives people the opportunity to say whatever they want with little, if any, filter.

Some people need excitement in their lives, so they try to "stir the pot" by being downright rude. Then they wait and watch to see how the world will react via the anonymity of the Internet.

What if all that energy was spent on something positive?

I got an email that simply said, "This seems like a good one for you if you're in need of some ideas."

Boy, was that person right! Below that one sentence was a series of photos, screenshots actually, taken of an entire conversation between a bunch of strangers on Facebook.

The first post was from a young man named Dustin who had gotten a new job but was still going to be $50 short for rent. He had one week to make up the difference, so he was asking if anyone knew of quick work – snow shoveling or yard chores – he could do.

People responded with all kinds of ideas, like donating plasma, being a pizza delivery driver, or contacting short-term employment agencies.

Then one woman bravely said this: "I know I'm just a stranger to you, but we are here to help our neighbors. I can give you a loan and you can pay me back."

And then 45 minutes later, the same woman came up with an even better idea and posted this:

"I know that there are many other people out there, like me, who would like to help but perhaps don't have $50 to give. Well, how about $5?

"That's all it would take, 10 people to give $5 in a 'random act of kindness' or 'pay it forward' gesture, and this man would be covered without anything to repay.

"I'll start... #1.

"Let's show everyone what North Dakota is made of. Who's going to be #2?

"Ready? Go!"

One minute later, she had her second donation. Four minutes later she had her third. In less than an hour, all 10 spots had been claimed by people wanting to help a total stranger.

The woman who came up with this brilliant act of kindness is Michelle Hjelden, a paramedic from Fargo. When I asked her why she did it, this is what she told me:

"I was simply compelled, by my faith and who I am, to act on behalf of Dustin.

"I know how warm a heart feels when you give selflessly. It makes me feel a warm, peaceful/soothing inner 'spark' that signals to me that God is pleased, and through that he makes me so much more thankful for what I have. The yearning to maintain that special feeling keeps me constantly striving to be a better person and keep that 'spark' aglow, because to be honest, not many other things beat it!

"I knew there were others on that post who also wanted to feel that way, but perhaps couldn't do it by themselves. I could have helped Dustin directly on my own, but I knew that many more people would be affected with that 'spark' if we all worked together by giving a little bit."

People whom Michelle had never met dropped off donations one by one. There were smiles and hugs and many warm feelings as Michelle recognized that special spark in each of their eyes.

And then, she got to give the money away.

"A young, timid boy ascended my stairs with his hands in his pockets, shoulders shrugged upward as if embarrassed, and head humbly bowed.

"He's a good kid who needed restored faith and trust in others, and he got it."

Dustin wasn't on the Internet looking for a handout. He was looking for odd jobs to make some quick cash to pay the rent. He got the money, but perhaps more importantly, he got the money wrapped in kindness, empathy and a vote of confidence with a gift tag that said, "We see you. We've been there. We know you'll find your way and help others in the future, but today, let us help you."

Thanks to one woman's clever idea, many people got to be part of something that was about much more than the money, and at the same time prove that the world – even on the Internet – isn't such a bad place after all.

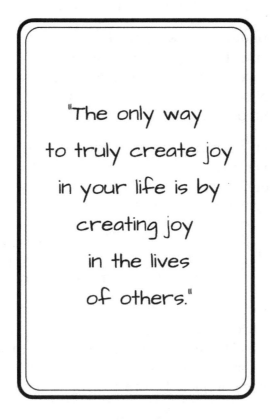

"The only way
to truly create joy
in your life is by
creating joy
in the lives
of others."

Kindness Reminds Us of Meaning of Christmas

My friend Liz has been haunted for a year by the way she reacted to her husband's random act of kindness last Christmas Eve. I'll let her tell you about it:

"I love the holidays. I look forward to them every year. But inevitably, I am always amazed at the amount of stress I feel during this 'joyous' season. So much so, that I become like a Christmas robot. If I stop, I might forget something, or even worse, run out of time.

"So, like most, I constantly shop, hide gifts, wrap gifts, plan meals, make crafts, try to keep up with the advent calendar, shop more, etc. Usually by Christmas Eve I'm so exhausted that I'm going through the motions and hoping for the best.

"Last year, after finishing some last-minute shopping, dressing my family in our 'holiday best,' and preparing food for Christmas Eve dinner, it was time for church.

"Knowing I would soon be singing 'Silent Night' in a candlelit sanctuary truly calmed me, although not enough. Still, in the back of my mind I knew that I had kids to put to sleep, gifts to wrap, breakfast items to prepare and many other Santa's helper duties to complete before dawn.

"Midway through the service, a man joined. He wore a hooded sweatshirt and carried a large backpack. It seemed as though this was his home, at least for the duration of the service.

"After the service, I smiled at him and hoped he was able to get some refreshments before he went on his way. I noticed my husband talking to him but didn't think much of it. After all, my husband talks to everyone.

"A few minutes later, my husband introduced me to the man and informed me that he was going to stay in our guest lodge that night. For some reason, my first emotion was anger. How could my husband put me on the spot like this?

"My next emotion was fear. What if he caused harm to my children? What if he stole from us? I also felt inconvenienced. Would I have to share my family holiday with this stranger? At what point would he leave? And where would we take him?

"In the heat of the moment, I pulled my husband to the side and tried to calmly and discreetly express my concerns through gritted teeth. However, my husband was determined to give this man a place to sleep on Christmas Eve.

"I begrudgingly got into the car with my husband, children and our new guest. During the long ride to our country home, I went through the list of things that I was going to say to my husband when we were alone.

"Meanwhile, he and this man quoted Scripture, spoke of Jesus and maybe felt the true meaning of Christmas (I wouldn't have known because I had abandoned the true meaning of Christmas weeks ago).

"Once we were home and our guest was settled into our lodge, I distracted myself with Christmas preparations. Soon, I heard my in-laws pull into the driveway. They came to take our guest to a hotel. A combination of guilt and relief consumed me. Why didn't I think of that?

"The next day, Christmas went on as usual. My kids were unfazed by the previous night's events and were overjoyed with the many presents Santa brought. A mixture of emotions was still swirling inside which left me feeling anxious and sad. I smiled and then cried when no one was looking.

"It has taken me almost a year to realize so many lessons from that night. If I don't stop, I might forget to see things like my husband does. He views the world with purity, kindness and light.

"I might forget that Jesus shows himself in many forms. He's not concerned about whether our shopping is done, gifts are wrapped or if the advent calendar is on the third or 22nd day. He's concerned about how we react in moments of need. To him, it's not about the kind of car we drive, but rather about who we give a ride to.

"If he ever shows himself to me again, I hope to act with more kindness. Luckily, I've got a great role model in my husband, who, in spite of my awful Christmas hospitality, still sees good in me every day."

Liz has been given the ability to see a difficult situation from a new perspective. It's an incredible gift that is worth taking an entire year to unwrap.

I hope you receive gifts that are equally as valuable this holiday season. Merry Christmas!

Santa Brings Gift of Kindness

I look forward to getting out the Christmas decorations each year and lovingly placing them throughout the house.

I usually pull out the boxes and turn on the Christmas music the day after Halloween, but this year I held off until the middle of November. My husband thanked me for my great self-restraint. As much as I love decorating, I hate un-decorating. The minute Christmas is over, I want everything out of my house. The same frames and figures I so tenderly set upon the mantle, I now throw into a box filled with crumpled up old copies of The Forum newspaper, which act as a nice buffer for my laziness.

When it comes down to it, my stuff is just stuff. Nothing holds much sentimentality because I have the great blessing of still being able to hold onto my little ones. I'm sure as they grow, I will find more meaning in those handmade ornaments labeled "Jordan, age 4."

My friend Judy has one very special decoration that I'm sure she finds difficult to put away each year. It's a snow globe, and it was given to her daughter, Charity, from a man who showed great kindness to both mother and daughter.

Here's Judy's story:

"I saw a man who played Santa at West Acres Mall in the 1980s who looked just like the storybook. He had that familiar squint that people get when they smile with their eyes.

"My daughter, Charity, was with her dad that holiday, so I skipped the Santa visit. When the next year rolled around, I went to the mall looking for that particular Santa. I was saddened to learn he had retired.

"When Charity was 5, she had been diagnosed with a heart condition called cardiomyopathy. It was a rough year as we learned about additional health complications. I wanted to make her Christmas really special.

"I did some research and found the name and address of that retired man from the mall. I sent him a letter, telling him I was a struggling single mom and that I couldn't pay him, but I could make him a good dinner and some really good cookies.

"He wrote back almost immediately saying he would be more than happy to play Santa.

"He came to the door with the few gifts I had left on the step for him to put in his big red bag to deliver to Charity. She was so excited to see him, and after she opened the gifts I had left, he pulled out one more. It was a gift from him. It was a snow globe with a Santa in the middle that played 'I'm Dreaming of a White Christmas.' Charity's eyes lit up, and she went to place it in her room.

"That night we formed a friendship with a Santa named Palmer Forness that would last a lifetime. Charity continued to write him, and we would exchange Christmas cards every year.

"We met for lunch in November 1997, two months before Charity died. We talked of old times and laughed. Charity put her arm around him and said, 'Palmer, I always knew you were the real deal.'

"Charity passed away unexpectedly in her sleep at the age of 16. About 750 people were at Charity's memorial service, and right there in the middle of this big church sat Palmer.

"When it was time to share memories, no one stood up. My heart was aching as I wondered why no one wanted to speak.

"Then, after what felt like an hour, Palmer stood up. He is rather shy by nature, so this was out of character for him. But he stood up and shared about that first Santa visit and many memories after in such detail that I found myself back there again. When he was done, everyone else wanted to share, and it turned out to be a beautiful night of memories.

"So as I've done every year since my first encounter with Palmer, I unpack the carefully wrapped Santa music box he had given to Charity years before. I wind it up and place it up high for everyone to see. I guess you could say I've always believed in Santa, but now I can say he's my friend."

You can learn more about Charity and cardiomyopathy, and visit an online support group for people who have lost loved ones at www.charitymae.com.

Kindness Thaws Frozen Boots

I want to teach my kids two things before I die: 1) the importance of being kind; and 2) the value of a dollar.

I want to teach them lots of other lessons, too, like how to drive a car and do their own laundry, but let's not rush it.

The kindness thing is important to me. When I find myself not being especially kind, I'll see my children's little faces and remember that they will do as I do, not as I say. They keep me in line, and we learn from each other.

The money thing is a little harder. My kids are growing up with so much more than I did, and I don't always think prosperity is to their advantage. I remember being a child and putting a winter coat on lay-away until my mom could afford to buy it. We had to make hard choices, but doing so made everything we got that much more special.

There is a woman in Fargo named Laura who probably feels much like my own mother felt when shopping. Tough choices have to be made, and when kindness enters the picture, it becomes all the more meaningful. Here is her letter:

"My 9-year-old daughter really needed church shoes and winter boots, so my children and I braved the post-Thanksgiving shopping crowds and went to Kmart.

"We found a cute pair of Disney 'Frozen' boots and a nice pair of black church boots. According to the sale sign, if you bought one pair of boots, you could get the other pair for only $1. It turns out the exception to the sale was the Disney boots. They didn't count.

"I asked a lady who worked at the store if she thought the 'Frozen' boots would count as the more expensive pair so the other pair would only be $1. No, she didn't think so. She smiled and said I should buy them anyway because they were so cute. I said I was planning on it, but money was tight and the 'Frozen' ones were $30.

"My 6-year-old son was asking for slippers, and the store employee heard me tell him 'no' to the pair he wanted. We moved over to the slipper/sock section to see if they had cozy socks that were more reasonable.

"The lady from the shoe department asked me if I was going to be in that area for a little longer and if I'd wait for her just a bit. A minute later, she came back and was talking to us about the boots and slippers and stuck some money into one of my daughter's boots. She said it wasn't much, but it was all she had in her purse and she wanted us to have it. I burst into tears! Even thinking about it now makes me weepy.

"This kind woman talked with the kids and me a little longer before she had to get back to work. When I looked at how much she had given us, I realized it was $30. I left that store feeling so blessed by a stranger's kindness." –Laura Hess Ronngren

Thanks for sharing your story, Laura. And thank you to the beautiful woman at Kmart who had a heart to send your daughter home with the perfect pair of boots.

In all you do and all you endeavor to teach your children, I hope kindness tops your list this New Year.

Face of Kindness Takes Many Forms

I was walking down the street with my 4-year-old son this fall when we came upon a young woman with a heavy limp using a cane.

As we approached her from behind, I could see his interest piqued and braced myself for whatever was about to come out of his mouth. I silently prayed that whatever he said would be too quiet for her to hear.

Nope. In full preschool buoyancy, he loudly proclaimed, "Mom! That lady walks funny." I wanted to crawl into a hole when she turned around. Until she smiled.

That young woman gave us the most beautiful smile and then said to my son, "Yep, it looks pretty silly when I walk. And I'm not very fast. I have a disease that makes it hard to use my legs."

We went on to have a brief but sweet conversation, and I left feeling so grateful for so many things, including her willingness to talk about the differences my son so obviously questioned.

A Minnesota woman who now lives in Colorado shared an experience she recently had in which kindness not only paved the way over awkwardness, but gave her a new friend.

"Traffic was backed up because of a tiny old lady, gingerly walking through the slush and ice, trying to cross the entrance of a parking lot. She was wearing a long blue jacket, thick mittens and good, heavy boots. She also had a paper mask covering her face.

"I pulled over and got out to help her navigate the sidewalk. I asked where she was going and if I could give her a ride. She was a little winded but managed to say, 'Light rail, train,

train,' which is about a mile down the street.

"After helping her climb into the van and buckling her in, she started thanking me profusely. She explained that she had missed the bus because her leg is sore from a skin graft. She isn't able to lift her leg high enough over the snow banks, and she is very afraid of slipping on the ice and breaking bones.

"She needed to go to the grocery store, so I told her I would go in with her, help her with her groceries and give her a ride home.

"Her name is Joan, and she is 82 years old. While I was helping her double-bag her four bundles of organic bananas, I couldn't help but notice the actions of the shoppers around us.

"Joan carried on as if not noticing the staring children, the avoiding glances, the startled reactions. You see, Joan doesn't have a face. She has piercing blue eyes looking out over a big rectangular skin graft covering where her nose, cheekbones, upper lip and upper teeth used to be. And she breathes through a tracheostomy tube.

"Bananas were the only things she needed, as they purée so well. She only eats what she can purée in her blender.

"On the way home, she told me how she had lost her face to 'the mildest form' of melanoma. She was originally diagnosed with it in 1965.

"When she was a young lady, she had gone to a dermatologist for her severely oily skin. Back then, they told her to sit in the sun to help dry her skin out. They also gave her sunlamp treatments, unaware that those were the worst things to do.

"Joan said she hopes there are no more recurrences because, she said, there isn't much more left of her face that they can take.

"But then she said, 'I am just so thankful to God that I am still alive.'

"When we got to her apartment, I carried her heavy bundles of bananas and walked her to her door. I wrote down my number and told her to call whenever she needed a ride or found herself in a pinch.

"I gave Joan a hug and went home.

"This remarkable moment in my life took about an hour to unfold. I am replaying it over and over again. I want to be sure to not miss any part of what I need to learn from this experience." – Marcy Bernier Corbitt

Friends Don't Need to Ask for Kindness

The strange yet obvious thing about moving to a new town is that nobody knows you.

When I moved to Fargo 10 years ago, I felt like I had moved to the "Twilight Zone." Never before in my life had I lived somewhere where I knew no one. My husband left the house and went to work each day, and I sat home with my infant daughter trying to figure out how to create a life that actually included other people. I remember going to a Starbucks grand opening. I went to the celebration simply because I wanted to be around people. I didn't even drink coffee.

I can't quite tell you where 10 years have gone, but I can tell you that I did eventually make friends and then became so close with those friends that I can't remember ever not being friends with them.

Thanks to my children, meeting new people in Ohio has been much easier. I have three kids who are involved in all sorts of activities that lead me directly to other parents with similar interests.

One of my closest friends here is named Liz. She has lived in Athens her entire life, so when she invited me out to dinner with her circle of friends, it was like some sort of social science experiment. I got to hear stories of who dated whose husband back in high school and how they snuck into the movie theater in college. These are women who have been there for each other through love, marriage and the baby carriage. It's truly beautiful.

Their bond is so close and so filled with acts of kindness that I don't think they even notice it. It's like breathing to them.

I happened to witness one of the most touching acts of

kindness I had seen in a while just because it came up as a side-note in conversation. Liz was telling me that she and a few other women had taken the previous day off work to hang out with their friend Becca, whose dad died in July. That mid-December day would have been his birthday.

I've met Becca before. She's either lighting up the room with her ever-present smile or sending the place into a fit of hysterics with some quick-witted, sarcastic comment. I immediately understood when Liz said Becca wasn't one to let people know something was bothering her. Becca subtly mentioned to her friends that she didn't know how she'd handle the day, that it would be hard.

That was it. She simply said it would be hard, and that was enough to round up the troops. Three of her friends took the day off work so Becca wouldn't have to be alone. I would be willing to bet there were several more women who wanted to be there but couldn't figure out how to play hooky without getting fired.

The friends went out for breakfast and then planned on spending the day shopping and watching movies, but no one ever hit the "play" button on the first film. They shopped and then spent the rest of the day sharing stories about Becca's dad and looking at pictures. Becca admitted there was some crying but said laughter and good memories quickly dried the tears. She also mentioned they discovered chocolate-covered potato chips. I was sure to tell her that we know all about those in Fargo.

Sometimes we spend so much time thinking we should be doing more that we don't realize how much we are already doing. Yes, I absolutely believe that we should pursue kindness and add it to our lives systematically and intentionally, but isn't it precious when we realize it's just a part of who we are?

An Extra Dose of Kindness Eases the Burden

I say that I'm grateful for my health and the health of my family. I say that I'm grateful for the food that makes its way to our table. But maybe I'm not.

Health and nourishment have always come easy. If I really knew what it was like to go without either, I think my gratitude level would change entirely toward both.

Perhaps there are some things that you can't truly understand unless you've been there, in the midst of the battle.

A woman named Fran is going through the battle with her husband. He's getting radiation at the Mayo Clinic in Rochester, Minn. Fran says she and her husband are counting their blessings because it's preventative radiation. But still, they are on the battlefield and they know what it's like. Maybe that's why their hearts were so touched when they encountered another couple who looked wounded and beaten:

"One morning last week after treatment, we went to the patient cafeteria for breakfast.

"While in line, we noticed a young couple ahead of us about to pay for their breakfast. When the clerk rang up their order, they didn't have enough money to pay for it. It just broke my heart to think that, here are two people, one most likely ill, and they cannot pay for their breakfast. The clerk made a comment that they could return something on their tray. I told the clerk not to worry, I would pay the balance of their bill.

"We got our food, paid for our orders and found a place to sit. I noticed the young couple went to sit in the farthest corner of the cafeteria, away from everyone. I sat there trying to figure out a way to make sure they had enough to eat. I was about to suggest we talk to the clerk when my husband said, 'Why don't you see if we can buy them a punch card or something?'

"I spoke to the clerk, and we were able to purchase a Mayo Clinic gift card they could use in any of the Mayo cafeterias. I walked over to them and told them they could use it anywhere in the Mayo System, trying my darndest to hold back my tears.

"When they left, they came over to our table and gave us a hug and a huge thanks. My hope is that when they are able, they can pay it forward. It doesn't take much to make someone's day a little bit brighter."

Even in the middle of their own concerns and expenses, Fran and her husband opened their eyes and their hearts to the needs of another couple. If they had simply paid for the extra food, it would have been helpful and solved the immediate problem, but taking the next step and loving those strangers enough to take a future burden off their plate took great kindness.

I can only believe the extra kindness they extended was good medicine for them all.

"Our vulnerability
is a great gift
to others because it
creates a safe space
for them to
be honest, too.
That's the space where
kindness lives."

Kindness is Both Courageous and Contagious

My dad is a deep thinker. He spent most of his life as a therapist, so he's a pretty good listener, too. He can be engaged in a conversation and then spend several days, if not weeks, thinking about the deeper meaning behind someone's words or actions. Had he not gone into the profession of family counseling, he would have made a great researcher in the field of sociology. Human interaction fascinates him.

My dad retired a few years ago and decided he'd had enough of Wisconsin winters. He and his wife now spend several months as snowbirds, swimming and playing shuffleboard at a condo in sunny Arizona.

He calls me on a regular basis to give me a weather report, find out if I need to take a last-minute trip out West, and to fill me in on the latest shuffleboard gossip. I wasn't at all surprised when he sent me this email. My dad had clearly been busy thinking again.

"Sometimes I think your column could be called 'Kindness is Courageous.' For men, it takes courage to do nice things for people. Probably for women, too, but especially for men. We wonder how our actions will be interpreted. Will people think I am showing off? Or if I do something nice for a woman, will she think I am trying to make a pass at her?

"In the last shuffleboard league game, I played a man who has suffered two strokes and now has limited use of his left arm. We were tied in the last frame when his phone rang. He was unable to get it out of his pocket before it quit ringing.

"He told me it was his daughter calling to see if it was time for her to come and get him. I called her back for him and therefore missed my last shot. He won the game. I took his phone and laughingly told her he won and she could come and pick him up. Andy was as happy as a pup with a new toy.

"My teammates, who were not on the same end of the court, didn't see what had happened and made several comments about me not focusing on the game. Kindness almost always carries a risk."

I agree, Dad, kindness almost always carries a risk. But so do so many of the amazing things we do in life – like spending every penny you have to go to college, like being the only single guy to sign up for country line-dance lessons, like teaching your teenage daughter how to drive, like asking a lovely woman on a first date. You've done risky things all your life, Dad. Why stop now?

Put Spark (of Kindness) Back in Your Love Life

Do you think of love in terms of passion and hearts and romance? Or do you see love as a test of endurance?

Does your love still sparkle, or have the lights gone out?

When Saul and I started dating, every moment was magical. He would look into my eyes and my stomach would flip. We thought nothing of driving seven hours every weekend to see each other. We got married because we knew, just knew, that nothing could ever come between us.

Shortly after we said "I do," our "Affair to Remember" became just "The Way We Were." Instead of surprising Saul with love notes, I started surprising him with new ice cube trays and the occasional package of socks.

What happened to us? Kids happened. Expenses happened. Jobs happened. In short, life happened.

I grew up thinking love meant passion and hearts and romance but somewhere along the way, it felt more like endurance.

Endurance is not an option in my marriage. While the word has great merit, to me, it is also a bit depressing. So every time I feel like we are backsliding or settling in or just enduring, I fight.

This year has been particularly hard. Being a basketball coach can be all-consuming. Being a basketball coach at a new school in a new town can feel like a whole new ball game. While I would say that our marriage is rock solid, there have been times this year when I've felt invisible. My husband is so focused on his job that it is occasionally the only thing he can see. I'm certain I cannot be the only wife out there who has ever felt this way.

Instead of further burdening him by complaining, I decided to spend my free time reading.

I chose the all-time fall back in love with your spouse book, "The Five Love Languages" by Dr. Gary Chapman. I was hoping to discover my love language so I could tell my husband, and therefore make his job of catering to my every need that much easier, since he's so busy. I'm a very good wife like that.

While I did learn that I especially appreciate acts of service and words of affirmation, I also learned that it's not about me.

I learned that truly loving someone is about putting that person first. It's about showing them you love them in a way they understand. It's about supporting them when they are preoccupied, holding your tongue occasionally, and doing things that you don't feel like doing just because you want to make their life better. It's about kindness.

The funny thing is, when I began focusing on my husband and what I could do to ease his burden, he began trying to ease mine. He started seeing me again. His job commitments didn't change. His stress level didn't change. But we were somehow closer. All of a sudden, we were in it together. And that subtle distinction made all the difference.

I think it's probably normal for the euphoria of love to ebb and flow during a relationship. Some days you may feel it and some days you may not. But if you've chosen to walk through this life with someone special, why settle for endurance when you can bring back the sparkle with kindness?

Kindness in an Easter Basket

The Easter Bunny stopped showing up at my house around the time my parents got divorced. I suppose it's no great tragedy. I was in third grade or fourth grade, and I was the youngest child in our family. At some point, it was just time for everyone to move on.

When I was about 13, my dad and I moved to a new town. By the middle of eighth grade, I had a made a few friends, but, in all honesty, I was still struggling to find my way.

I was a teenage girl living with a single father. My life was full of angst, both real and imagined. Tragically, that was the year I attempted to commit suicide. Since I'm sitting here today writing this column, I can say with great certainty and gratitude that God had other plans for me.

One of my most distinct memories from that year happened just before Easter. I was sitting at the school lunch table with my friend Colleen. I think we were talking about something incredibly important, like our favorite types of candy.

Colleen started asking about my family's Easter traditions and what I thought I'd get in my basket. When I told her it had been several years since the Easter Bunny had paid me a visit, Colleen's jaw dropped. "You don't get an Easter basket?! How can you not get an Easter basket on Easter?"

I went on to explain the difference between her family and mine. While it's true that she lived with two parents, I think the biggest difference was that she was also the oldest child in her family. She had younger siblings who were still in elementary and preschool. Of course the Easter Bunny would still show up at her house.

Even after my lengthy monologue, Colleen still couldn't

envision a time in her life when there would be an Easter morning without an Easter basket.

Lunch was over and we left the cafeteria and the conversation. I didn't think anything more of it, until a few days later, when I got called down to the principal's office.

Sitting on the secretary's desk was the biggest Easter basket I had ever seen. It was huge and colorful and filled with deliciousness, and it was for me.

I stood there in shock. Who would do this? I asked the secretary who had delivered it, but she would only say that it was from the Easter Bunny himself.

I can't tell you how loved and cared for and even protected I felt at that moment. It stands out in my memory as one of the greatest random acts of kindness I have ever witnessed. And it was all for me.

Colleen refused to admit that she had anything to do with the basket.

Looking back, as a mom myself, I can almost see how that story would have unfolded: Colleen coming home from school and sharing our conversation with her mother, the two of them hatching a plan to create this surprise, and then running to the store to buy an extra basket and loads of my favorite candies, finally pulling it all together by delivering the gigantic gift to the school office and begging the secretary not to tell.

One of my sweetest memories happened because another girl listened. Then her mother listened. Then they both cared. That's how kindness unfolds. That's how people are lifted up. That's how we change the world.

Moving Kindness

Being a coach's wife has its perks. I got to take my kids to the NCAA Men's Final Four basketball tournament this past weekend in Indianapolis.

For most people, it's a once-in-a-lifetime experience. For the Phillips kids, it's part of Daddy's job. Sometimes I wonder if my children will ever realize they live a life many middle-aged men would trade their left foot for.

Anyway, while I should have been focused on the teams and the hype and the fanfare, I was stuck in a land called Nostalgia.

I kept thinking about how one year ago, at this same tournament, my husband accepted a job that would start the next chapter in our lives.

I was reminiscing about the whole whirlwind of our move to Ohio when a family friend said, "You should really put together a to-do list for other moms who need to move."

What a great idea! I immediately put everything aside and made my list. Here it is: Surround yourself with good friends.

That's it. Just make sure you have a circle of personal cheerleaders so when the going gets tough (or your husband decides to take a new job), you have people to lead you through the chaos.

I had friends in Fargo pack my suitcase, take over taxi duties for my children when I was too exhausted to wiggle, and even coordinate the sale of my house. They showered me with kindness during my last six weeks in North Dakota.

When I got to Ohio, God's greatest gift to me wasn't the nice house or the good schools or the warmer weather; it was the people. After only a year, I am humbled to say I have a group of friends who love and protect me like a mama bear protects her cubs.

But before those friendships were formed, I relied on little acts of kindness from strangers to help me get through each day.

An online post from a woman who recently moved to Fargo reminded me of how fortunate I am to now be surrounded by such close friends.

This woman didn't have a support system in place when she made the move to the F-M area, but she soon felt the kindness of the community.

She posted this thank you note on the website reddit.

"I just want to say thank you so much to the angel at the gas station who helped me. I don't know if you'll see this, but thank you... Thank you so much for giving me $20. When I asked you for some gas, I was flat broke and my tank was empty. It means the world to me. I'm a single mother of two sons and these little things help. We moved here from out of state. I had just gotten a job, but our fridge was empty, our gas tank was empty and I'm not going to see a paycheck for another two weeks. What you did for me was truly a blessing."

The responses that came after that post were extraordinary. People from the Fargo area offered to have pizza delivered to her door, sent her the address and hours of the emergency food pantry, emailed her Walmart gift cards, and offered to donate clothes to her boys.

The outpouring of kindness included this message, "I'll meet you at a gas station and fill up your gas tank the rest of the way. I'll come wherever it's most convenient for you. If I don't get back to you right away, I'm sorry. I work the graveyard shift so I might be asleep, but I will get back to you."

And this one, "Moving is stressful. Let me know of a couple of restaurants in town where you and your boys would enjoy eating. I've got you covered for dinner and a movie! I'll send some e-gift cards if that's cool with you. Welcome to Fargo!"

Can you even believe there are people in this world who would go so far out of their way to help a stranger? I can only imagine that at some point, someone, somewhere, helped them out in their time of need, and now they are giving back, proving again that kindness is contagious.

Kindness Reveals True Beauty

They say a picture is worth a thousand words. Well, I only have about 500 words to work with, so let's hope that's enough to draw a picture.

I saw a video online that I can't get out of my head. It was produced by the Dove company as part of the "Choose Beautiful" campaign. In the video, there are two doors side by side. Above one door is the word "Beautiful." Above the other door is the word "Average." Both doors led to the same place, but for some reason women had trouble walking through the door labeled Beautiful.

This little experiment was done in San Francisco, Shanghai, Dehli, London and Sao Paulo.

It isn't just American women who struggle with self-concept. Women from these five major global cities stood outside the doors contemplating which word fit them best. In most cases, they ended up walking through the door that signified they thought of themselves as average.

Halfway through the video, something really piqued my interest. Women with their daughters or friends literally stopped, changed courses, and urged the person next to them to walk through the Beautiful door. They chose to put their own self-conscious feelings aside to instead remind their companion that they are indeed beautiful. In that one moment, the women chose kindness.

One mother interviewed said she wished all young girls would see themselves in a more positive and powerful light. That's why she wouldn't let her daughter walk through the Average door.

Another woman who was pushing a friend in a wheelchair

stopped and veered over to the Beautiful door when she realized she was about to walk through Average. She wanted her friend to know she thought she was beautiful.

I have a friend who is struggling with some major stress right now. She says at the end of the day, all she wants to do is drown her exhaustion in potato chips. She is feeling fat and ugly. Neither of those words fit her in the least.

Not sure how to lift her spirits, I simply sent her a text that said, "You are beautiful. I just thought you should know that, since clearly the enemy has been filling your head with lies."

This is not even about physical beauty. It's about seeing yourself as you truly are: wonderfully made, a miraculous creation both inside and out.

But often we can't see that for ourselves. That's where kindness comes in. It takes nothing, we sacrifice nothing, we lose nothing, by telling someone we think they are worth more than whatever this world is offering them.

Some people live in homes where they are constantly surrounded by love and uplifted with positivity, but some people don't. You may be the only person who ever thought to tell a friend or stranger that they are special.

That's powerful. That's kind. That's beautiful.

"It's not important
that we give kindness
to the right person.
It's just important that
we act on what
tugs at our heart.
As long as
kindness happens,
it can continue to be
contagious."

Kindness Isn't About the Money

I used to think kindness was all about the money. Boy was I wrong. Anyone can walk by a beggar on the street and throw some coins in a can. But the person who stops, kneels down, looks that beggar in the eye and says, "Hey, I care about you because my creator cares about you" is the person who truly unveils the power of kindness.

My friend Ann sent me this touching story. She says the experience wasn't about the money, it was about the message.

"It had been a long day. I worked and ran lots of errands before arriving at the library to support a friend who was having a public art show. It was an amazing opportunity for her and I wanted to be there to share in her joy. But man I was tired.

"As I was waiting for the event to begin I noticed a young man sitting on a bench outside the library. He was wearing a sweatshirt and sweatpants and the only skin I could see was his tattoo-covered hands. His head was hanging low. Texting fast and steady, he never looked up the entire time I was watching him. Who was he waiting for? He had a story and I guessed it was a hard one. He just looked sad.

"When I came out of the art show, I noticed he was still there, sitting all alone with his phone. He hadn't moved in over an hour and a half. I started to pass and then I just couldn't. My legs stopped in their tracks. I quietly asked, 'Are you doing okay, sir?' He looked up with a startled face and answered quickly, 'Um. Yeah.'

"I told him I noticed he had been sitting in the same spot for over an hour and wondered if he was waiting on someone. He explained that a friend had planned to pick him up, but

224

now couldn't. He had been texting his mom who lives a few hours away in Columbus asking her what he should do. He knew no one, didn't know the area and wasn't sure how to get home.

"I reached in my purse and pulled out three $5 bills. I handed it to him and told him there was a cheap commuter bus which travels between Columbus and Athens once or twice a day.

"I said to him, 'Look at me. Tell me you will use this money to take the bus home.' He stared in disbelief. His eyes filled with tears. He took the three bills and said, 'Are you an angel?' He seriously was so shocked by the generosity that he meant the question.

"I looked straight in his broken eyes and said, 'I am not an angel. I could be exactly where you are right now. If I got what I deserved I would have absolutely nothing. Nothing! God had mercy on me, and when I gave my life to him, he took the broken pieces of my life and fixed it. I am blessed beyond measure. Not an angel, but a follower of Christ. Turn from whatever path you are on and follow him. Things will get better.'

"He said, 'I've been sitting here for hours asking my mom, what can I possibly do to get out of this situation? I have no one. No one cares for me. How did you know I needed this money to get home? Why me?'

"I pass people with little signs every day. Homeless. Hungry. Need help. I look and I pass. I don't intend to ever hand money out to a drug user. Not always are we led to act. But sometimes we are. Sometimes we need to allow the God of all creation to move in someone's life even if you don't know why. Do what the Spirit says to do. Obey. It might not be about food or bus money. It might be about a lonely, desperate young man, who just needs to be told and shown he is worth it.

"As I got up to leave, his hand reached for mine. 'I'm Rob,' he said with a smile on his face. 'I'm Ann. I'm praying for you tonight, Rob, that the bus will get you home and that God will bless you and keep you.'

"I'm glad I was kind. It felt good to know the gift I gave him had nothing to do with money."

Kindness and My Breast Cancer Diagnosis

"You've done a lot of acts of kindness today, Mom." I seriously cannot get anything past my 11-year old-daughter.

I had just hopped back in the car with a Diet Mountain Dew that I picked up at the gas station for a neighbor.

"What do you mean, Jo?" I honestly couldn't think of any act of kindness I had done besides the current one.

"Well, you just bought that soda for Cathy and earlier we dropped off shoes for Ashlyn and before that you took me to JoAnn's to pick out fabric for Michelyn."

Oh. Right.

My daughter had just cracked my code: On days when my spirits are low and my anxiety over the future is high, I start overdosing on acts of kindness. It's like medicine to me. The more things I can do to brighten someone else's day, the more energy and positivity I pump into my own body.

I just found out I have breast cancer. My doctor says we caught it early and with a little (or big) surgery, we will be able to fix this thing.

Here's the backstory: I turned 40 on May 7 and, like I do every year on my birthday, I went in for my annual check-up. The doctor felt a lump that I had never noticed. She sent me in for an ultrasound, then mammogram, then MRI and then a biopsy. Before I even got the diagnosis, I knew it was breast cancer. I could feel God whispering to me that everything was going to be OK and that he was going to use this experience to help other women.

If you don't have this type of relationship with God, I understand it may sound strange to hear that I was hearing from the Great Almighty, but I'm telling you, that's just how it worked for me.

Most days, I am filled with an incredible peace and joy (yes JOY!) as I am being loved up by my friends and soaking in each suddenly precious moment with my family. However, every once in awhile, fear creeps in. It fills me with lies and starts my heart racing. And that's when I turn once again to kindness. Intentional, systematic, courageous kindness. I go out and look for ways to brighten other people's days.

It's like my own private form of chemo—only there are really no negative side effects. Sure, it may cost you a few bucks. And it may take up a few minutes of your perfectly timed-out day. And you may get a strange look from the recipient of your kindness. But the return on your investment is priceless.

If you don't believe me, try it. The next time life overwhelms you, send out an encouraging email to an unsuspecting soul, or buy the silly magnet that reminds you of a friend and deliver it to her or him, or pick up a soda for the lady who lives next door. Be random. Go off script. Do something no one would expect you to do. Take a risk. Be courageous in your kindness.

It's the most healing medicine you could ever take, for whatever ails you.

An Act of Kindness Could Last for Generations

We've all been there, in line at the grocery store, when either we came up short or the person in front of us did. Maybe that's why last week's column about the woman who paid for the elderly man's groceries resonated with so many of you.

In the past week, I've been delighted to hear your stories. Each act of kindness is precious and unique. I'd like to share two of them with you now.

The first is from Alden Sprecher, who lives in Mapleton, N.D., and works at the Village West Hornbacher's store.

"Last week around noon, a young lady in her 20s stopped at our deli for some lunch. She only spent about $3.50 or so, but when she swiped her card, it was rejected. She tried two or three more times with the same result.

"Almost immediately, the next lady in line said, 'Let me pay that for her,' which she did, and the young lady thanked her for her generosity. When the transaction was finished, I thanked the lady myself. She said sometimes people just need to be shown a little kindness.

"Many times I've taken some money from my own pocket to help a customer who is short some coins, but sometimes I don't think fast enough. I could have swiped one of my own credit cards and helped the young lady, but to my shame, I didn't. I felt embarrassed myself."

Thanks for sharing your story, Alden, and just think, if you had quickly pulled out your own money, the other lady in line would not have been given such a special opportunity to save the day with kindness! I bet she walked out of the store feeling renewed and energized by her ability to help another woman in need.

Here's another grocery store story that really touched my heart. It's from a woman named Jessica.

"My grandpa, John Julius Novotny, passed away two years ago at the age of 92. He served in the Korean War, raised six children in a small home, and worked as a butcher at a neighborhood grocery store called Churchill's for more than 50 years. In fact, after he 'retired,' they called him back to work, less to actually cut meat and more to just talk to the customers. He was a humble man and prayed on his knees every night until he couldn't get down on his knees anymore.

"I knew he was a great guy, willing to give the shirt off his back to anyone who needed it, but someone told a story at the funeral that really made me stop in my tracks.

"A man in his late 50s walked up to the podium. He said when he was a kid, he was sent to Churchill's for some ham, but he had already spent the money, so he was stealing the meat. My grandpa caught him in a corner. The guy was sure he was going to call the police. But instead, my grandpa pulled out his wallet, handed him a $5 bill, and said, 'If you want the ham, you can't just take it. Now go pay for it. And if you ever need anything again, come to me.'

"As a butcher with six children, my grandfather didn't have a lot to give, but yet he still gave a lot. This story and my grandpa's legacy of kindness have inspired me many times to do the kind thing."

Thanks for sharing your story, Jessica. How long will our acts of kindness make an impact? I guess we never really know. It could be something people talk about for generations to come.

Give Yourself and Others Some Grace

I don't even care that I have breast cancer right now. I really don't. Do you know what I'm distraught about? I'm grieved that the parents of two Park Christian students had to bury their sons this week. I'm grieved because it feels like the entire nation is divided over recent decisions by the Supreme Court. I'm grieved because a man in Fargo, 10 blocks from where I used to live, was killed when he answered the door to a guy asking for a glass of water. I'm grieved because nine people were killed in South Carolina during a Bible study. I'm grieved because I got an emergency phone call from the police department stating that a minivan was stolen with a child in the backseat.

Enough. It is enough.

I want to lock my whole family in the house and refuse to let anyone in or out.

I want to stand on top of a mountain with a megaphone and scream for everyone to just BE KIND.

But since neither of those options will produce the results I'm longing for, I will do the next best thing. I will be kind. Me. *I will be kind.*

I will simply do what I can today to make the world a little bit better for the people around me. I won't worry about what the fallout will be from smiling at a stranger or giving money to a neighbor in need. I will just do what I can do today.

We live in a free country where we can set off fireworks and buy guns and worship or not worship. That kind of freedom comes with risk. We are like children who are given a taste of adulthood and get to pick their own bedtime or eat as many treats as they'd like. But as we know, that sort of freedom means we have to pay bills and act responsibly, or we will wind up needing a nap and aching from too much sugar.

What I am trying to say is this: None of us has mastered life. We all get it wrong just as much as we get it right. So give the people around you some grace. When they are hurting because they have lost a child or a friend in some senseless accident, sit with them. Don't worry about taking a side or getting angry on their behalf. Simply sit in the uncomfortable silence until it becomes comfortable. There is no "right thing to say," so don't worry about saying anything. Let your kindness speak for you.

When politics come between you and a friend, ask yourself, "Is it more important to be right or to salvage this relationship?"

Again, I implore you, give others some grace. We never know what path they are walking. And while you are at it, give yourself some grace, too.

Fighting Cancer with Kindness

I've held the belief for a while now that if you truly want to be happy and feel fulfilled, you have to get your mind off yourself and onto the needs of others.

Constant introspection makes your problems bigger, your pain more acute and your life pretty dismal. When you can get out of your own head and your own little world, and fix your focus on the needs of the people around you, your troubles become less troublesome.

At least that's my theory.

Cancer has given me a unique opportunity to test out that theory.

There have been plenty of days when I have wanted to accept the invitation to my own personal pity party. To be honest, there have been plenty of days when I have.

But not every day. Most days I fight the urge to go down that black hole using my No. 1 weapon: kindness.

I remember one day, early on in my diagnosis when I was haunted by dark feelings. I just couldn't escape myself and my sad/angry/spiteful attitude. I was being particularly ugly to my children and my husband, who had no choice but to stand there and take it. Mom has breast cancer, after all. We wouldn't want to upset her by gently pointing out that she is being a nasty beast.

Anyway, I was driving down a street a few miles from my home when I noticed a woman my age whom I'd seen around town. She was homeless, but living in a tent in a neighbor's yard. I had picked her up a few times and driven her to wherever she was going.

On this particular day, she was walking along the side of the road. I pulled over and rolled down my window. "Hi! Need a ride?"

She thanked me, but declined.

My fiercely independent new friend had just gotten a job that required her to wake up at 4 a.m. so she could walk several miles to get to her job before her 6 a.m. shift started.

For several nights in a row, I had been lying in bed in the wee morning hours listening to the thunder and thinking of my friend walking in the rain.

Now, today, I was face-to-face with her and I had a choice. I could ask her what I was thinking or I could let her fend for herself.

Even in my growly mood, I chose kindness.

"Are you still walking to work? Do you need me to drive you? Or pick you up after your shift?" I asked.

"Actually, I'm saving up for a bike," she replied.

All of a sudden, a lightbulb went on. I told her to stop by my house and pick up the extra bike that was sitting in my garage.

That evening, she shyly walked up to my house to retrieve the bicycle.

"I'll bring it back as soon as I get paid and can get my own."

"No," I said. "It's a gift. I want you to keep it."

She stood looking at me in a state of total disbelief.

I went on to explain that I had noticed how hard she had

been working to get her life back on track. I told her she was an inspiration to the people around her, including me.

She didn't know quite what to say as I stood there desperately trying to speak life into her soul. With tears streaming down her face, she gave me a hug.

All of a sudden, I didn't have cancer. I didn't have a black cloud hanging over my head. I didn't have a feeling of ugliness painted like tar across my lungs.

I was light and I was free.

I had tested out my theory on kindness, and it was true. When you get out of your own head and fix your focus on the needs around you, your troubles become less troublesome.

Kindness Can Clean Up the Biggest of Messes

I had the strangest thing happen to me the other day. Someone totally burst my kindness bubble, and I was left standing in the middle of my bedroom wondering if I should scream, cry or just go back to bed and pretend it never happened.

I was home, recovering from my mastectomy surgery and unable to do anything for myself. Literally, I was told not to lift anything heavier than a can of soup. No pouring my own milk, no putting dishes in the dishwasher, no scrubbing down kitchen counters.

Perhaps you can imagine with three active children in the house how incredibly sticky and gooey a home can become in a few short hours. Well, it had been two weeks since my house had seen a vacuum or a washcloth, so in a pinch, I took a suggestion and called a cleaning lady who came highly referred by a good friend.

The day of the cleaning arrived, and I was beyond excited to see the woman arrive at the predetermined time. I walked her through the house and showed her where everything was and explained what needed to be done. I left her a check for $125. Expensive, but this was going to be an all-day job.

I thought it would be best to just get out of her way for a bit, so my girlfriend drove me uptown to get my hair washed, since that, too, is something I couldn't do on my own.

Just over two hours later, I returned home.

Maybe you can guess what happened, but I would never in a million years have imagined that a person could look me in the eye, agree to do a job, and then basically take the money and run.

Yep. I'd been had.

I called the woman and asked if perhaps she was out having lunch and planned to return soon to complete the job.

She sounded confused and then said, "No. I finished the job. Well, my son got sick so I had to leave, but I finished the job."

Let's just say that the conversation deteriorated from there. I may have, in my very kindest voice, asked her to explain exactly what she had cleaned since I could not see any strong evidence of her existence.

I hung up the phone, not proud of myself and not proud of people in general. All of a sudden, the world, and everyone in it, including myself, looked very, very dark.

I stood in my bedroom trying to figure out what to do next. Should I cry? Should I scream? Should I head back to bed? Someone I didn't even know had offended me, and I was coming unglued.

I have learned that you are supposed to pray for your enemies, and at that moment, that lady felt like an enemy. So I prayed. I asked God to show me both my behavior and her behavior from his perspective. I asked him to forgive me and to forgive her. I asked him to make that horrible feeling in my stomach go away. I never thought he'd use kindness to answer my prayer.

At just that moment, the back door opened, and I heard the the voice of my 5-year-old son who was hanging out with his favorite babysitter for the day. They were not supposed to be home for another four hours, because I was supposed to be sleeping and recovering from surgery.

Babysitter Kelsey took one look at me and said, "What's

wrong?" I spilled the whole story, while Ben ate his lunch and Kelsey listened sympathetically. Then she said, "You need to sleep. I'll take care of it."

Four hours later, when I walked out of my bedroom, still feeling groggy from sleep and painkillers, I smelled oranges and lemons and freshness.

My house was clean. From top to bottom, every inch of my house had been turbo-cleaned in four hours by the world's best babysitter (I also call her my friend) and her 5-year-old sidekick.

The horrible feeling in my stomach had been replaced by immense gratitude.

Now, when I think of that day and that cleaning lady and my not-so-kind behavior, all I can think about is the amazing power of kindness to turn something bitter into something beautiful.

Kindness is Not Put on Hold

I was speaking at an event recently when a woman raised her hand and asked me, "Have you found that kindness truly is contagious?"

What a great question. The answer I gave her was a resounding "Yes!" but I struggled to come up with an immediate specific example. Sometimes kindness comes directly back to us, and sometimes it's passed on to the next person. There are so many stories, so I was embarrassed when my mind wouldn't work quickly enough to filter through them all and find just one to share with the group.

I thought of that question when reading a story from my friend, Tania, about her trip to the grocery store. Tania is the type of person who has a smile and encouraging word for every person who happens to cross her path, whether she knows them or not. She found out the kindness she has been spreading is indeed contagious. Here's her letter.

"Often we hear that kindness given will be returned to us, but seldom is it immediate. Today, it was immediate for me. I was running behind at the grocery store and rushing to check out. There was only one lane open.

"I had a full cart, so when I noticed a lady get in line behind me with only two items in her hand, I motioned for her to go ahead. She thanked me and went on. Then, as I continued to unload my cart of goodies, another older woman came up, asking if I minded her going in front of me because she only had one item and a friend was waiting for her. I've been the recipient of kindness too many times in my life to forgo this small gesture, so I said 'of course,' and on she went.

"Finally, it was my turn. Halfway through, as the cashier was ringing up my large amount of items, I felt this sinking feeling in the pit of my stomach. I realized I didn't have my debit card. This particular store accepts only debit or cash, and I had neither.

"I looked at the cashier and confessed, expecting I would have to slink out of the store in embarrassment (as there was now a long line behind me to witness my transgression). Immediately though, she said she'd finish ringing my order, call the manager to put the order on hold for later, and wheel my cart in the freezer to keep it cold. That would give me time to run home and get my card.

"I looked at her with gratitude in my eyes, believing I was receiving kindness because I'd given kindness. I promised a quick return and headed out of the store, believing this to be the end of my kindness moment. Yet, God wasn't done giving me a wink (as a friend of mine so lovingly puts it).

"I was almost to my car when the store manager came out after me. He walked up to me, stated that he'd personally pay for my order, so I could take it home, if I'd only come back later and pay him back.

"For what seemed like too long, I simply stared at him. I couldn't believe he was offering to do this for me. I said thank you, got my bags, and headed home.

"My heart was full of gratitude and clarity. I'd said 'hi' to this man every time I'd entered his store, never expecting for anything to come of the simple act, but today something did. Kindness does come back around and everyone does understand it. Needless to say, this gentleman's kindness was quite unnecessary, but it didn't go unnoticed and it will be returned many times over."

Thanks, Tania. It's pretty amazing when we get to give and receive kindness, when all we planned to do was buy groceries.

Be Kind Like Mister Rogers

I am cancer-free! My husband and I wistfully joke that someday we'll look back and say, "Remember that summer I had breast cancer?" It'll be just one more little chapter in the story of our lives.

I'm still going through the process of reconstruction, so I have at least one more surgery in my future, and I'll have to take an anti-cancer pill for the next 10 years, but believe me when I say, I know I got through this about as easily as possible.

The words "thank you" don't seem big enough to fit all of the gratitude in my heart. The Fargo Fercho YMCA sent me an enormous get-well-soon card, Hope Lutheran sent me a prayer shawl and ruby slippers, and the president (yes, the president) of North Dakota State University personally sent me flowers. Twice.

My kids started teasing me about getting "fan mail" because so many cards filled with words of love and encouragement arrived at our door.

I have never felt so cherished, lifted and protected, even in the midst of something as scary as cancer. Thank you.

But now summer is over and I'm restless, a little anxious even. I feel more called than ever to reach people with the message of kindness. It feels more like my ministry than ever before.

The problem is, after something as big and bold as cancer, kindness seems kind of plain.

Cancer was constantly evolving in my life and in the lives of the people around me. It was all new. I was seeing its many aspects for the first time, and I was caught up in the swirl of doing something dramatic.

The attention brought on by the cancer left me thinking, "Kindness? Who really wants to hear about kindness?"

And then we went on a family field trip to Pittsburgh. You might know it as the home of the Pirates and the Steelers, but Pittsburgh was also home to a man with multiple homemade sweaters, blue canvas sneakers and a motorized trolley.

"Mister Rogers' Neighborhood" was filmed in Pittsburgh.

Walking through the Children's Museum of Pittsburgh, I got to see the sweater and the shoes and the characters from the Neighborhood of Make Believe. The 5-year-old girl inside of me came alive. All of a sudden, I saw Fred Rogers through eyes filled with both adult scrutiny and childlike wonder. I saw a man filled with love, joy, peace, patience, kindness, goodness, faithfulness, gentleness and self-control.

Rogers didn't set out to be famous. He didn't set out to save the world. He didn't even set out to change people's minds. He simply did what he loved to do and knew to be right. And after doing it day after day after day, people started listening.

Maybe you are passionate about something. Maybe you feel like pounding your head against the wall because people are not falling in line with your way of thinking. Or maybe you think your opportunity has passed you by.

Let me assure you, as long as there are people in this world for you to love, your opportunity has not come and gone.

In the words of Rogers, "You're the only person in the whole world who's exactly like you. Isn't that wonderful? The same is true for every person you ever meet. Everyone is unique... and special."

Do what you know to be right, day after day after day, whether anyone notices or not. Don't worry about being exciting or important or well-known. Just be kind. Like Mister Rogers.

Using Your 'In' for Kindness

Allow me to step back in time just a bit as I lead into this story on kindness.

It was May 2014: After 10 years in Fargo, my husband accepted a job taking us to Ohio. We made the emotional decision to pull our children out of school and transplant them in Athens before the end of the academic year so they would have time to meet other kids before the summer break.

Jordan was in fourth grade, and Charlie was in second. Both kids put on brave faces as they said goodbye to their Fargo friends and looked with anticipation toward our next adventure, but I knew they were scared. How could they not be? I was scared for them.

My children's first day at their new elementary school happened to coincide with Grandparents' Day. As divine intervention would have it, Grandma and Grandpa were in town helping us move into our house.

My momma heart could not have been any more grateful, knowing that my babies were going to find their new teachers, classrooms and classmates while holding the steady hand of a much-loved grandparent.

Teachers know that not every student has a grandparent available, so those kids get to invite a special friend instead. But when my in-laws came home after school that day, they told me that some of the students had nobody. No grandparent. No special friend. No one to listen to their poem. No one to compliment their artwork. We all just kind of shook our heads and made comments like, "How sad."

This year, I got to be the special friend for all three of my kids. I was pretty sure I'd be one of the younger guests in attendance, so imagine my shock when I walked into a lobby filled with college students.

Nearly 35 members of the men's baseball and women's basketball teams from Ohio University had given up a day to be the surprise guests of their youngest fans.

You should have seen the kids' faces light up when those athletes walked into their classrooms. Instead of being a day to swallow tears of loneliness, this became a banner day forever etched into many a young child's mind.

I was standing in line at the book fair when I noticed a young man talking to several eager kids. I think the boys came up to his waist, but it was hard to tell because they were sort of hopping around. They couldn't stand still, they were that excited. When it was time to pay, the baseball player pulled out his wallet and used his own money to buy each child a book.

Grandparents' and Special Friends' Day was about one incredible act of kindness after another, and it all came about because one woman saw what my in-laws saw and decided to fix the problem.

RaeAnna Smith has been to a lot of Grandparents' Days. Her twin daughters are in high school now, but she still has kids in the elementary school. RaeAnna said it always made her sad to see the kids alone on Grandparents' Day, so this year, she thought she'd do something about it. She used her "in" as the wife of the Ohio University baseball coach to convince the athletes to come to the school.

We all have an "in" that could make the day a little better for someone else, but how often do we use it? How often do we use our cooking skills to help out the neighbor who eats dinner alone? How often do use our free time to watch the child of an overburdened mother? How often do we see a need and think, "What can I do to help?" instead of simply saying, "How sad."

I want to be more like RaeAnna. I want to be a person who looks for the solution, or at least the part of the solution that I can provide. You can be that person, too. All it takes is a little kindness.

Listen to the Little Voice in Your Head

I let an opportunity for kindness pass me by, and I still regret it. I was at a restaurant when the server mentioned that she liked my necklace. A quiet voice in the back of my mind was nudging me to give it to her, but a louder voice was telling me how silly that would be and how uncomfortable that interaction would be for both of us.

Now, let me tell you, I am a person who listens very closely to the little voice in my head because time and again it has led me to do things that have changed my day, and my life, in ways that I couldn't have imagined. Like writing this column — that was a little-voice moment — and many of the stories I share with you come from little-voice moments.

So, I'm embarrassed that I let the big, mean voice win out. Especially when I read a letter sent in from a woman in Fargo who was indeed gifted with a necklace in a restaurant, and just what that gift meant to her.

"I had the most wonderful experience. I was the recipient of a random act of kindness, and it brought tears of joy and gratitude to my eyes.

"I am a middle-aged woman who has been downsized twice in the past three years from a professional and highly sought-after position in an industry that has experienced much change. I decided after the last downsizing to try my hand at being a server. I haven't been a server for over 35 years, so it was an unusual choice for me to make.

"I almost gave up, thinking I would never get the table and seat numbers correct, much less catch on to the nuances of the menu or the computer system. Once I figured it out and gained confidence in my ability to do the job, I discovered I liked the work and it gave me a sense of accomplishment. I was raised in a large family with a mom who cooked dinner for us every night. She showed her love and kindness by preparing and serving us food, which may have something to do with the sense of satisfaction I get from serving food and doing my best.

"My incredible experience came from the last table of the night, which was a family of six with two adult daughters. I complimented one of the daughters on her necklace, and she thanked me. As they were leaving, she took her necklace off and gave it to me. She said she had gotten enough use out of it and she wanted me to have it since I liked it so much.

"These people were strangers to me, yet their 21-year-old daughter felt the need to give me her beautiful necklace! I was so touched by her kindness and generosity, I sobbed after they left. I had been having a rough day thinking of my beautiful older sister who is suffering from Alzheimer's disease and my mom who passed away from the disease a few years ago. My mom was the type of person who was generous and kind, like this young woman, and I could envision my mother giving her necklace to a perfect stranger. The kind and generous act done for me by this young, caring woman felt like a message from my mom, that she is still with us and that everything will be OK."

You never know the battle someone else is facing and what your act of kindness may mean to them. May I suggest we all start listening to the little voices in our heads?

Be Kind By Choosing Compassion

I find it interesting that we teach our children the importance of using manners and being kind and standing up for others, but sometimes we as adults fail in our own actions and words. I'm as guilty as the next person of hustling by someone who looks different. I avoid eye contact for fear that they will ask me for something I don't want to give.

Yet, when I slow down and make that connection, I am always rewarded. So what about the times I choose not to slow down? I think there is an opportunity to be kind, even in those circumstances, simply by keeping our negative thoughts to ourselves.

Listen to this story sent in by a woman from Minnesota.

"Nicole, I also strive to show kindness in my daily life as I work in a small-town grocery store and know many of my customers by name. Something happened recently that has impacted me a great deal.

"I was on the till when I saw an obviously homeless man stop outside our front windows. He painstakingly tied his dog up behind our large hedges so no one could get close to or bother his pet.

"While he was doing this, a customer stopped to talk to him. They conversed for a few minutes and before parting, the man pulled out his wallet and handed the man with the dog some cash.

"It was several minutes later when the homeless man came into the store. He shopped for maybe five minutes and then proceeded to the checkout. He was a nervous guy and said he was surprised that someone had been nice enough to pick both him and his dog up and give them a ride. I don't know where he came from or where he was heading, but I do know he was nervous about being separated from his dog and wanted to check out quickly.

"While he was getting his dog and packing his groceries, I heard people around me making comments that were not kind, and it made me so angry. People seem to instantly judge someone who is homeless as being dangerous or dishonest. This man is someone's son or brother and maybe he was a war vet. It's possible he has a mental illness. It is not our place to judge someone, but to help if possible.

"I was so grateful to the man who stopped and talked to him and gave him some money. I thought about this situation for the rest of that day. I have taught my children to help those who are less fortunate, and I hope there are many more people in this world, like the man who gave him money and a ride, that cross the paths of the people who need them."

Not everyone who entered that store was called to give something to the homeless man. We all feel a tugging in our hearts for different things. But imagine the children entering the store that day with their parents. In that instant, even with no money changing hands, we are given an opportunity to teach our children to lead with either judgment or compassion. I hope for the sake of the next generation, we choose compassion every time.

Some of the greatest advice ever handed down came from the movie "Bambi," and a little bunny named Thumper, who reminded us that momma always said, "If you can't say something nice, don't say nothing at all."

"Kindness
is like medicine.
Two a day
keeps the doctor
away!"

My Daughter Fights Cancer with Kindness

I know a little girl whose momma had breast cancer this summer. As soon as the diagnosis was announced, that young lady, though she was just 11, set out to do whatever she could to spread kindness throughout the house. She helped her daddy with chores, kept peace with her brothers, and delivered food and water to her mother when she was too weak after surgery to get out of bed.

Although she was doing so much, the little girl wanted to do more. That's one of the problems with cancer. It has a way of making us feel like we're never doing enough. Until the person we love is cured, cancer fills us with nervous energy that tells us we need to keep moving... even when we're 11 and it doesn't seem like there is much we can do to help.

This little girl loves to sew, so one day, right after the mother's second surgery, the little girl asked her mom if she could sew something to sell in hopes of raising money to help other women with breast cancer.

An idea was born: Cozys for the Cure. The little girl set up a webpage through the Susan G. Komen foundation and started sewing lots and lots of coffee cup cozies.

One night, the mom put a link on her Facebook page, and by the next morning that little girl had raised more than $500. Within two months, she was $150 shy of reaching her goal of $3,500.

Her momma agreed to give one more shoutout on Facebook. The $3,500 goal was met within 15 minutes, but over the next 24 hours, hearts were moved to continue giving. In all, more than 100 people donated to the cozy cause and $4,500 was raised.

This story is special to me, but difficult to write because it's the story of my family. That little girl is my daughter, Jordan.

Cancer wanted to steal, kill and destroy, and there were moments when it felt like it might be successful. But like any form of adversity, what doesn't kill you makes you stronger.

Without cancer, my daughter would have never gotten to see the generosity of an entire community. She would never have learned that a big impact comes a little bit at time. And she would not have felt the pride that is born from being the top fundraiser in a philanthropic event that included more than 1,500 people.

Jordan raised enough money to provide more than 40 women with mammograms. If the statistic holds that one in eight women will be diagnosed with breast cancer—and early detection is the key to saving their lives, then my daughter has spared dozens of other children the tragedy of losing their mothers.

The scars on my chest will forever tell the story of my summer with breast cancer, but thanks to the generosity of people in North Dakota, Minnesota, Wisconsin, New York, Ohio, Florida, the Carolinas and California—and the one little girl who brought them all together—those scars also tell a pretty special story of kindness.

Use Kindness to Find Meaning

Do you ever wonder why you're here? I know I do.

People need purpose. I'm at my best when my gifts and talents are being put to good use; when I'm on the right track.

I'm guessing I'm not the only one who feels this way.

Rick Warren's book, "A Purpose Driven Life," is the best-selling book of all time, second only to the Bible. Is that because Warren is the most talented writer ever? Maybe, but I think it's more likely that his success is based on his ability to tap into and talk through a question we humans continually ponder: What on earth am I here for?

Viktor Frankl said he survived the Holocaust because he found personal meaning in the horrific experience. He used his skills as a physician and therapist to help other concentration camp prisoners process the trauma. He went on to write a book called "Man's Search for Meaning" in which he said, "Everything can be taken from a man but one thing: the last of the human freedoms — to choose one's attitude in any given set of circumstances, to choose one's own way."

He also included in that book these poignant words, "Those who have a 'why' to live, can bear with almost any 'how.' "

The times in my life when I have been most deflated were the times when my brain asked my heart questions like, "Do I matter? Do I really have a reason for being on this planet, or am I simply taking up space? And if I am here for a purpose, then how do I find it?"

What do purpose and meaning have to do with kindness? For me, it's all intertwined. Kindness has everything to do with purpose, because kindness was my avenue to purpose. We think we need to have a long-term plan set in place, that our life marathon needs to be totally mapped out before we take the first step, but it doesn't work that way.

Let's flip that illusion and instead of thinking of the end result, think only about the method. How will I reach my ultimate goal of being filled with purpose and meaning?

I suggest we begin by being kind. Courageously kind.

Let go of the continually ticking stopwatch and the heaviness of burdens and the pull of duties and choose instead to see someone else's load. Then think, what can I do right now to make that person feel significant? Can I surprise them by paying for their coffee? Can I send them a quick note telling them what a great job they're doing? Can I ask them in passing how their day is going and then slow down enough to actually listen to the answer?

Kindness becomes powerful when we make it an intentional part of our day, every day.

When you are systematically kind, you get to walk around knowing that you were the highlight of someone's day. Their day was better because of you. That's pretty heady stuff.

The mean girl in my head still goes back to those questions sometimes. I get tired or discouraged or beat down by the day and wonder, "Do I matter?"

Then I think back and recall the look of surprise or gratitude on someone's face as I added a little light to their sphere, and I know the answer.

As long as I am living with the intention of making life better for others, I am standing in the midst of my purpose. And so are you.

Choose Kindness Even Without the Applause

My daughter asked me a question the other day that on the surface seemed kind of childish and selfish. Yet, it's something that, even as an adult, I still wrestle with in my mind and in my heart. She said, "Mom, what do you do when people don't recognize your kindness?"

Jordan went on to explain there is a girl in her group of friends who seems to need a little extra love these days. Always one to pounce on a challenge, Jordan started daily acts of service. She gave up her seat at lunch, which meant sitting with other classmates at a different table. She bowed out of a group project with two close friends so this girl could take her spot. She is making it her mission to find ways to make this girl feel special and included, even when it means taking a backseat to her own desires.

It's the very essence and definition of kindness, and I'm as proud as a momma peacock.

The problem is, this other girl isn't acknowledging Jordan's kindness. She isn't being mean, but she also isn't saying "thank you" or offering sacrificial kindness in return. She's just sort of going on with her life. Which leads my daughter to ask, "Mom, what do you do when people don't recognize your kindness?"

That's a tough one. The older she gets, the more these questions seem to appear. Why do people act certain ways? Why doesn't that person like me? What can I do to change this situation? My sweet girl will soon enter the land of teenagers and the stakes will continue to grow. Each question carries more weight. How am I supposed to teach her what I am still learning?

I took a deep breath, prayed for wisdom and jumped in.

I was honest. I told her I understand her question because I often ask myself the same thing. There are times when I give someone something and they don't say "thank you" and it bugs me. I have given people pricey presents only to find out they have re-gifted them to their dogs. I sometimes reach into my wallet and wonder if the person I'm giving to will expect more in the future.

When I start having those thoughts, I check my motives. Why am I helping that person? Why am I giving that gift? Do I want to be elevated somehow? Am I hoping to make them like me? Am I hoping others will see me and know I'm super-duper amazingly generous?

Or does my gift come from a place of gratitude? Am I so filled with love and thanksgiving that it can't help but overflow onto the people around me? Do I give because I love others or because I want to be loved?

The difference is crucial.

If you are looking to be loved and accepted by other people, your kindness will always fall short. The power of kindness doesn't come from an outside reaction, it comes from the spark of energy that ignites inside of you when you work to make someone else's day brighter.

It's called "giving" because we must let go. We must do the kindness that our hearts prompt us to do, and then walk away, knowing that we fulfilled our responsibility. The outcome isn't up to us.

If we feel like we are being taken advantage of, then perhaps our hearts will prompt us not to give to that person in the future, and that's okay. We just can't allow our brains to park in a spot where we are discouraged or perturbed.

The last thing I reminded Jordan (and myself) is that we are all human, and as humans, we love to be applauded. It's in our DNA. So when it seems like no one notices, let me assure you, they do. I have people whom I have never done anything thoughtful for who say to me, "You are so kind and you have such a kind family."

Kindness is never wasted. It makes your day better, it makes your character stronger, and even if it's not being acknowledged by the recipient, it's being noted by someone.

So what do you do when people don't recognize your kindness? Love on. The applause is just a bonus.

The Kindness of Sacrifice

One of the best things about having three kids in elementary school is that I get to spend a lot of time as a fly on the wall. Some people call it "volunteering," but I call it "pretending to work while I'm secretly spying on my children."

I got to be part of a very special event at the school recently. It's called Santa's Workshop. Area crafters set up shop in the gym for the day, and each class, kindergarten through sixth grade, takes turns shopping for members of their families. Some kids bring money from home, but even those who show up empty-handed are given a few dollars to make a special purchase.

The big kids are pretty good at budgeting their money, but the little ones need a helping hand, so I got to play the part of an elf for a morning and assist in the shopping experience.

Let me tell you, there is a lot you can learn about a 5-year-old in 30 minutes. Some kids came in looking to buy something "for Pops, who's in prison" or "my big brother, who doesn't drink beer anymore."

It's heartbreaking and endearing all at once. Those kids love their people without judgment, and they want their people to have a Merry Christmas regardless of what else is going on in their complicated lives.

There was one little girl whom I was especially delighted to assist since her mom and I are friends. Her name is Zara, and she is a pint-sized Mary Poppins. She is equal parts playful and precocious, and to put her delightfulness right over the top, she speaks with a British accent. Her parents are from England and moved here eight years ago, before Zara was even born, but the little girl has picked up the amiable lilt from her mother.

Zara came prepared with a well-thought-out shopping list. Each member of her family was listed, along with something they might like to find under the tree. Unfortunately, our mission was side-tracked at the first table when Zara spotted a bracelet that was absolutely screaming her name.

"Oh! I love this! This would be perfect for me!" Zara exclaimed. I gently reminded her we should probably buy for the people on our list before we chose something for ourselves.

Zara was having none of that. In the most regal (yet squeaky) voice possible came this British declaration, "It is the exact colors I adore, and it's my perfect size." Then, turning to the woman running the booth, announced, "Yes, I'll take it."

I giggled to myself and had to grudgingly admit that it did look adorable on her.

After that, we settled into the serious business of finding treasures for her sisters. Zara chose matching coin purses and then pondered which sister would like which pattern the best. After making that difficult decision, we moved on to a gift for her father. That one was easy. Zara picked up a bag of chocolates and said, "He loves sweets."

Zara found one or two more things to tuck under the tree for herself, then we headed over to the bagging station to wrap the presents.

She had just pulled out the last gift when I made a terrible realization. Zara was out of money and we had forgotten to buy something for her mother. Her mother, who is my friend, whom I should have most definitely remembered. Yikes!

I was just about ready to run to the car for my purse when Zara pulled the most selfless act of kindness I have seen in a long time.

As I explained we had neglected her mom, she paused, looked me deep in the eyes, and then said almost dismissively, "No we didn't! I got her this bracelet, remember?" And she took the coveted bracelet off her wrist and handed it to me. I set it gently on the tissue paper and began wrapping.

Zara may have loved that bracelet, but it could never compare to the love she has for her mum. In one small moment, I was reminded by a kindergartner that it really is better to give than to receive.

Replacing Jealousy with Gratitude

I have a problem with other people's successes. There, I said it. It's out in the light. Take it away, God. Rip this pride and jealousy and ego and selfishness out of my life from the roots. It has no room to coexist with kindness.

I get great inspiration from female speakers and authors. Women who are moms, just like me, who are writing, just like me, breathe hope into the dark places of my life and remind me that other people wrestle with the same issues I'm trying to pin.

But the entire time I'm reading their blogs and books, I have a pinch in my heart. How do they come up with these perfectly turned phrases? How can they string so many eloquent statements together that it becomes a brilliant new book series or viral blog post? And why can't I do it?

That's the sticky spot. Clearly they have something I don't have, and in my most shameful moments, it makes me mad.

Do you ever feel that way? Do you ever ask yourself questions like: Why does she have money to go on vacation when I don't? Why can she get away with eating ice cream every night and I can't? Why does her marriage seem so much more fulfilling than mine?

Am I alone in the boat here? Maybe your thoughts are different than mine, but I bet you have them. Or perhaps you're at the spiritual level that I'm aiming for and have already uprooted all the nastiness from your life. If so, please teach me. When does the breakthrough come?

Just before Christmas, one of my children was struggling with the ugly cousin of jealousy. Selfishness. As much as we would harp on the child to lose the selfishness, it was still quickly becoming a regular guest in our home.

After about four days, it occurred to me: The best way to lose a habit/mindset/behavior is to replace it with something else. You don't tell a smoker, "Well, just don't smoke." You have to give them something else to focus on until the craving passes and eventually a more productive habit takes its place. So that's what we did.

I marched down to the basement, got waist-deep in a closet that really needs to be de-cluttered, and emerged with five tiny notebooks in hand.

Gratitude journals. Every night we spend a few minutes privately reflecting on our day and then writing down five things for which we are grateful. The kindergartner in the household gets help from mom and dad — I think last night he was grateful for five separate bathtub toys. The big kids are on their own. No judgment. No grading scale. Just write what comes into your heart.

You know what I've noticed? We aren't using the "S" word nearly as often. And Mom needs this gratitude journal as much as the kids, because it works for the "J" word, too. When I force myself to sit down and form the letters that form the words, I am able to see that we are all given gifts. Specifically, we are all given different gifts. I may or may not have any sort of viral blog post in my future and you may or may not have a renewal in your marriage, but if you look at the examples other people set and say, "It can be done!" instead of "It can only be done by them," you'll have much more room in your life for kindness.

The Kindness of Mrs. Johnson Lives On

Every once in awhile, a person comes into your life just for a season. We'd like it to be longer, but the gift we were given has an expiration date, and for one reason or another, the time comes when the season has ended and the person is gone.

Shortly after I started writing this column back in 2011, I got a letter from a 90-year-old woman. The previous week, I had written about how hard I was finding it to raise three small children and maintain a kind demeanor, especially in my home.

This woman, with great wisdom, gently reminded me to let the sticky fingerprints and the dirty floor go. She told me to relax. She told me I was a good mom. She didn't even know me, and yet with that one letter, she breathed life into my weary soul.

The next time I got a letter from Mrs. Johnson, she included a $50 check. She told me she greatly valued my words about kindness and wanted to show me in a tangible way.

The third letter I got from Mrs. Johnson included a request: may she write letters to my children?

And that's when the season of kindness truly blossomed.

I have two large manila envelopes filled with nearly 100 letters sent back and forth between Mrs. Johnson and my now 11-year-old daughter, Jordan.

Jordan would tell Mrs. Johnson things like how spooky she thought our basement was, and Mrs. Johnson would tell Jordan about how she used to have to churn butter in a cellar with a dirt floor and that she would take her dog along for protection from the shadows.

Jordan told Mrs. Johnson about the lunches at Longfellow Elementary, and Mrs. Johnson would write back and tell Jordan about her one-room schoolhouse in rural North Dakota, and how each morning she would put a potato by the fire and by noon it would be baked and ready for lunch.

We visited Mrs. Johnson at her North Fargo home several times. Jordan would sit right next to her on the couch. I have no idea what they talked about, because they kicked me out so they could have some "girl time."

Before we left, Jordan would always run over and give Mrs. Johnson just "one more hug" about three more times.

We all cried when we visited Mrs. Johnson for the last time before moving to Ohio. We knew we'd keep on writing, but we also knew we'd never see each other again face to face.

Several months after our move, the letters stopped. By this time, Mrs. Johnson was 94. I imagined she was in heaven, and I looked in the obituaries for confirmation, but I could never find her name.

Finally, just last month, I found out that indeed our season with Mrs. Johnson had ended.

I got an email from her daughter explaining the decline in her mother's health and her eventual passing. I was so grateful to have closure. Mrs. Johnson's daughter sent me a DVD of the funeral service, and it was through the words of people who had known her much longer than I that I got to hear things about Mrs. Johnson that surprised me and yet, didn't. The depth and width of her kindness extended far beyond my comprehension.

Mrs. Johnson's letters serve as an instructional manual on how to love others in an unlovable world. Her check for $50 hangs in a frame on my office wall, still uncashed, as a reminder that you can't put a price on kindness, and that someone I didn't even know believed in me and my mission.

It's sad to lose a friend, whether through death or other circumstances, but it's better to have had the gift, even for a short time, than to never have had the gift at all.

I look forward to seeing you again, Mrs. Johnson, in a place where we can continue to let our friendship blossom in a season that will never end.

In Conclusion...

When I first started writing the *Kindness is Contagious* column, my husband gave it six months. He (lovingly) figured that within half a year, I would either run out of material or run out of passion for this new project. As a wife who looks for every opportunity to prove her husband wrong, I'm happy to say it's been more than five years and there is no end to kindness in sight. I have the world's happiest email inbox, and I'm more passionate than ever, for both kindness and my husband.

I guess if I had one thing to say about kindness, it would be that I wish I had discovered the truth about it sooner.

I had wrongly assumed that kindness was something that came from my surplus: extra time, extra energy, extra money. If I didn't have enough for me, how could I possibly have enough for others?

It wasn't until I broke out of that mentality that I realized I had it all wrong.

Kindness is like a secret passageway that God uses to bless us while He's blessing others.

"You're blessed when you care. At the moment of being 'care-full,' you find yourselves cared for." Matthew 5:7 (Message)

It's my prayer that reading these stories has inspired you to create kindness stories of your own. But beware! I'm certain kindness has the power to transform *your* life, because I've seen it transform mine.

Thank you

I would like to thank the following people for making this book a reality:

*Bill Marcil, Jr., publisher of The Forum of Fargo-Moorhead; thank you for seeing me as a writer even when I didn't.

*Cris Linnares, Women's Impact Founder & champion friend

*Mary Jo Hotzler, Heidi Shaffer & Sherri Richards, the fabulous Forum editors who worked on these stories.

*My Best Yes Girls who covered this project with prayer.

*A very special thank you to my early reading team, who read every word of this book (even the ones that didn't make sense). Teresa South, Stacey Piechowski, Gretchen Locy, Andrea Coombs, Galo Kostka, Judy Simon, Cheryl Backsen, Beth Kern, Sherry Pekas, Christina Willison, and Katie Hasbargen, this book would look a whole lot different without your valuable input!

*Saul- You are my everyone. You are the kindest man I know, especially to me. I love you.

* Jordan (12), Charlie (11) & Ben (6) Phillips -You are the reason I want to be kind. I hope this book will serve as a reminder in life that the goal is not to be perfect, the goal is to be kind. I wish I was a good enough writer to explain how very much I love you.

*The people of Fargo-Moorhead and those throughout the country who have allowed me to share their stories in hopes that kindness truly becomes contagious!

About the Author

Nicole Phillips is a champion for using kindness to overcome all of life's difficulties, including her own battle with breast cancer. She spreads the message of the healing power of kindness through her public speaking and weekly column, "Kindness is Contagious" which runs in newspapers in North Dakota and Minnesota. Nicole has her Broadcast Journalism degree from the University of Wisconsin and has worked as a television anchor and reporter in Milwaukee and Madison, Wisconsin and Fargo, North Dakota. As Miss Wisconsin 1997, she spent the year touring the state talking to children and adults about overcoming crisis. She was probably 11th runner up to Miss America that year, but we'll never know because they only announced the Top 10. Nicole lives in Athens, Ohio, has three children and is married to Ohio University Men's Basketball Coach, Saul Phillips.

Submit your own stories of kindness at info@nicolejphillips.com or catch up on Nicole's latest kindness columns and blog at www.nicolejphillips.com.

Printed in the USA
CPSIA information can be obtained
at www.ICGtesting.com
LVHW022229210923
759002LV00032B/775